WE LOVE FOOTBALL

AF399276

Football is the most popular game in the world. Place can not be found in the world where it is not played.

Eusebio: "Anyone can play whether you are poor or rich. All you need is space and a ball"

Football players and coaches are known from colorful language. Most of the quotes in this book are hilarious.

Zlatan: "Now I'm here, I think the people in Paris will have something else to see besides the Mona Lisa"

Quotes can be also paradoxical.

Luis De Agustini: "Gaddafi's a great bloke. The media only show the bad things. I used to go round his house. His son's a super simple guy. All the Gaddafis were very down to earth"

Some of them tell about own feelings.

Mwepu Ilunga: "I did not have a reason to continue injured while those who will benefit financially were sitting on the terraces watching"

Many of the sayings are very inspiring as well.

Messi: "Talent and elegance mean nothing without rigor and precision"

I hope that these quotes will make you laugh and inspire your day.

Enjoyable moments
Adrian Adams

© 2014
Kustantaja: BoD – Books on Demand, Helsinki, Suomi
Valmistaja: BoD – Books on Demand, Norderstedt, Saksa
ISBN: 978-952-286-908-1

Aad de Mos

"I will also take risks in the future. At least, it is good for everyone... our team, the crowd and also the opponent"

Abbas Suan

"Sport is the shortest route to peace. We will do what we can and we hope that the politicians will do the rest of the job"

Abedi Pele

"To see another Pele being born would be difficult. Perhaps there will be a player better than Pele, one similar to Pele, but a new Pele is impossible. My father and mother have stopped the machine"

"Character alone cannot push the ball inside the goal"

Ade Akinbiyi

"I was watching the Blackburn game on TV on Sunday when it flashed on the screen that George (Ndah) had scored in the first minute at Birmingham. My first reaction was to ring him up. Then I remembered he was out there playing"

Ademar Pimenta

"In my opinion, Brazil will only play in future in America because we traveled 10,000 kilometers only to have hassles!"

Adil Rami

"Now there are lots of boot-lickers who don't say things to your face. That's why things aren't going well between me and (coach) Dukic"

"We need to keep our head and show our balls"

"My favorite actresses? Eva Longoria, Eva Mendez, Megan Fox, Shakira"

Adrian Mutu

"I am not afraid of the beautiful women in England who, I hear, chase after footballers"

"I didn't take cocaine. I took something to make me feel good"

"I am not hooked on drugs. I categorically deny this"

"I now know who are the ones who are just with you for the good moments and those who leave you or turn against you immediately you are in trouble"

Ahmed Hassan

"I will play against Niger to remove any doubts regarding who is the most capped player"

Ahn Jung-hwan

"I am sorry for Italy, but I play for the South Korean team. The Italians only know how to win - not how to lose"

Aidy Boothroyd

"We don't have them (players) growing in greenhouses out the back because we don't have time for greenhouses. We're more of a microwave sort of club"

Aki Riihilahti

"'Don't you know who I am?' won't get you into nightclubs"

Alain Perrin

"The closer we get to the end of the window the more clubs raise the price of the players and try to force us into paying more than we should"

"I am impatient... we need to get the ball in the net, not the allotment!"

Alan Brazil

"Levante have gone fourth in Serie A. If anyone can tell me what part of Italy Levante is in, please call. I've no idea"

"Paolo Di Canio is one picnic short of a hamper"

"Some of the Scotland players need to look themselves in the face"

Alan Brown

"Soccer is the biggest thing that's happened in creation. It's bigger than any 'ism' you can name"

Alan Hansen

"You won`t win anything with kids"

"As a boy I was torn between two ambitions – to be a footballer or run away and join the circus - at Patric Thistle I got to do both"

Alan Pardew

"Sometimes you want (Gabriel) Obertan to open his legs and do something a bit exciting"

Alan Shearer

"One accusation you can't throw at me is that I've always done my best"

"Sometimes going in for a hard tackle generates a louder cheer than a great pass"

"Andy Carroll will cause anyone problems and I don't see a problem in that"

"If you take the money away, a lot of the footballers would still be playing football. So, the money has nothing to do with it"

"Football's not just about scoring goals - it's about winning"

Alberto Garcia Aspe

The coach (Manuel Lapuente) said they could only beat us by getting balls into the box, and that's exactly what happened”

Alf Ramsey

"The missing of chances is one of the mysteries of life

”I am not one to jump over the moon or off a cliff”

”Did I play when the USA beat England in the 1950 World Cup? - I was the only one who did”

Alfredo Di Stéfano

”No player is as good as all players together”

“Reputations do not win matches and trophies, only goals can do that”

”I retired at age 40 because my daughters looked at me one day and said: ´Dad, being bald and wearing shorts doesn´n look good together´”

Aleksandr Kerzhakov

”Winning a championship is a mark of quality for any sportsman. That can`t be taken away from you”

Alessandro Altobelli

”I want to thank my parents for my career, especially my father and mother”

Alessandro Del Piero

”I haven't got a regular place in the Italy team. I'm not guaranteed one just because my name's Del Piero"

"My ambition is football itself not the money I'd make from it”

Alessandro Diamanti

"I would have moved to a big club only because people said I couldn't move to a big club"

Alexander N'Doumbou

"Competition is healthy"

"I do not have the habit of judging myself"

Alexandre Pato

"Am I going to be a virgin when I get married? No, I`m not Kakà"

Alexandru Epureanu

"Each of us has the potential much higher"

Alexandru Baltoi

"I dedicate this goal to Ionut Badea who this morning gave birth to a little girl, so i dedicate this goal to him"

Alex da Costa

"Heurelho! (Gomes), guess who`s PSV`s new captain? Me - I finally got the armband"

Alex Ferguson

"That lad (Filippo Inzaghi) must have been born offside"

"They say he's an intelligent man (Arsene Wenger), right? Speaks five languages. I've got a 15-year-old boy from the Ivory Coast who speaks five languages!"

"I can't believe it. I can't believe it. Football. Bloody hell!"

"You know Dennis Wise. He could start a fight in an empty house"

"When an Italian tells me it's pasta on the plate I check under the sauce to make sure"

"I do believe in fate"

Alex McLeish

"The more you lose, the more you don't win"

"We want to win the match in 90 minutes, even if we have to go to extra time to do it"

"I look forward to hearing from the silent majority"

Alex Song

"When my children see Leo Messi, they try to emulate him"

"On the pitch, you don't just need one leader. You need them in every position"

"If you want to be a professional footballer you need to trust yourself and give your best"

"Forget Barca, Arsenal have given me everything. If I had to leave, I'd break down and cry"

Alexei Mikhailichenko

"I couldn't see Rooney's tackle from my position - but I assume it was quite dangerous and ruthless"

Alexi Lalas

"I'm living proof of the impact the World Cup can have on someone. It changed my life"

"In my job as a commentator it's helped understand decisions that maybe the fans can't"

Allen Bula

"It's definitely been a long road (For Gibraltar to EURO 2016)"

Alon Mizrahi

"It amazes me that all teams in the eighth-final (EURO 2004) are European"

"I want to play either in Europe or in Spain"

Alvin Martin

"If Arsenal don't finish third, they might not finish in third place"

Amadou Moutari

"I am patient and waiting my time"

Amarildo

"Once I saw that Pele could barely walk during the game, that's when I started thinking what it would be like to replace him"

Andre Santos

"Very good win gays!"

Anders Lindegaard

"The first thing that happened when I came is that I was put on a diet. In short, they told me I was too fat"

Andrea Pirlo

"After the wheel, the greatest invention in history is the PlayStation"

Andreas Möller

"Milan or Madrid. I don't care as long as it is somewhere in Italy

"My problem is, that I am always very self-critical, even against myself"

Andrés Guardado

"I learned to live life, what they do not teach you in school"

"The world still thinks Mexicans are brown dwarfs, with a mustache, drinking tequila like water and eating tacos"

Andrés Iniesta

"Football isn't a science. We play this way because it suits us"

"I do not play to win golden balls , I play to be happy"

"Some people like you, some people don't. In the end you just have to be yourself"

"I get the feeling people respect me and that there is affection for me. That makes me happy"

"Perfection doesn't exist"

"Individual prizes are not important"

Andriy Ševtšenko

"I feel less adrenaline in my body now, but more in my head"

"If my goals and victories can help the world remember Chernobyl and bring a smile to the face of the people who are still suffering - I dedicate all my success to them"

Andy Gray

"Darren Fletcher is the type of player who would walk over hot coals to play for his country, and he has done"

Andy Najar

"Where I lived, there was only soccer"

Andy Ritchie

"One of the coaches at Brighton used to make us play 5-a-side without a ball. I scored best hat trick you´ve ever seen"

Andy Townsend

"I think one of these teams could win this"

"Liverpool are going to have to start getting results if they're going to start winning"

"Freddie Ljungberg desperately wants to suck in Cocu"

"In the end, (Tomáš) Rosický initially did well"

Ángel Cappa

"The ball is the only one who does not sweat in a game, so run it"

Angelos Charisteas

"We're the champions of Europe. I believe this is a unique moment, which many of us may never experience again"

Ante Razov

"When you get a chance to whack it, you whack it"

Anthony Baffoe

"I do think it's important that I have moments of German directness. Nine o'clock is nine o'clock, not ten past nine. We can do it! That's exactly what I'm trying to get across, and it's gone very well up to now"

Antonio Rattin

"My team mates advised me to visit the city first. I went to have a look at Middlesbro and decided I was better off in Parma"

"I sat in the rostrum of the royal carpet. British threw beer cans at me. And I do not like English beer"

Antonio Valencia

"I repeat that it is not easy for a new coach at a club used to so many years Alex Ferguson on the bench"

"We really couldn't understand our results this season. It was all like a bad dream and we had to change the whole outlook"

Antti Niemi

"I've been training for just over a month now but for the first two weeks of that I couldn't even catch flu"

Arda Turan

"Messi or Ronaldo best player in the world? In the world, I would say Ronaldo. Messi is from another planet"

Arild Stavrum

"Tired after practice I had a shower. I put a lot of soap on and after opening my eyes I realised that I was the only naked man among 10 Turks wearing shorts. Then a German entered the shower and I was happy. I doubt that Elton John would be happier than me to see a naked young man"

Arjen Robben

"It's (Lakeside darts venue) close to where I live, so I was curious to see it from a close distance"

Arrigo Sacci

”I never realised that in order to become a jockey you have to have been a horse first”

"We couldn't even score against a team of journalists"

Arsène Wenger

”If you eat caviar every day it´s difficult to return to sausages”

"You weren´t world-class when Arsenal signed you"

”A football team is like a beautiful woman. When you do not tell her so, she forgets she is beautiful”

"Ferguson should calm down. Maybe it would have been better if he had put us against a wall and shot us”

“I banned the players from stuffing their faces with chocolate. On the bus, the players chanted ‘we want our chocolate bars’”

"I don't kick dressing room doors, or the cat - or even journalists"

"I haven't seen it, but it looks generous"

“We do not buy superstars, we make them”

Artuo Lupoli

"I have had to adapt to a different footballing mentality since I have been in England. I got booed by the crowd the first times I fell to the ground under challenge. In the eyes of English people all Italians are divers, and there is an element of truth in that. I think back to one of my former coaches, who taught me to run in a particular posture so I would go to ground more easily"

Asamoah Gyan

“Although my mother who advised me not to take penalties for Ghana is no more, that is the last thing I have to do to pay my final respect to her, so for now I still stand by my decision not to take penalties for Ghana”

"Some players go home and play golf, I sing. I sing from morning to evening!"

"I have been the country's lone striker for the past six years, it shows how great I am"

Barry van Galen

"The game had to be played in the afternoon, because the boys from Ajax aren´t allowed to play outside when it´s dark"

Barry Venison

"I always used to put my right boot on first, and then obviously my right sock"

"The Croatians don't play well without the ball"

"Romania are more Portuguese than German"

Bebé

"One day I passed the ball through Ryan Giggs' legs and Alex Ferguson said 'go and tell your mother you did that to Ryan Giggs'"

Benjani Mwaruwari

"I had my heroes, and now, I guess, I am a hero for some of the young boys playing football in Zimbabwe. And I know it's important for me to lead by example"

Benni McCarthy

"The World Cup in 2010 is going to be the most inspirational thing ever to hit the streets in South Africa. The biggest players, from all over the world, will be playing football in a stadium just round the corner from home"

"He's (Jason Roberts) like a second wife"

Benoit Assou-Ekotto

"When I started playing football I had only one objective - to become rich quickly and stop football more quickly"

Benson Mhlongo

"I don't spray champagne, I drink it"

Bernard Lacombe

"I don't talk football with women. That's how I see things. They can go back to their saucepans"

Berti Vogts

"If I walked on water, my accusers would say it is because I can't swim"

"They will try to hit anything that moves, so our midfield should be safe"

Bhaichung Bhutia

"I feel you should know where to draw line of finishing in every sport"

Bill Nicholson

"It is better to fail aiming high than to succeed aiming low. And we of Spurs have set our sights very high, so high in fact that even failure will have in it an echo of glory"

Bill Shankly

"Some people believe football is a matter of life and death. I can assure you it is much, much more important than that"

"The only way Everton players will get into Europe this year is if there's another World War"

"There are two great teams on Merseyside; Liverpool and Liverpool Reserves"

"I would have played Tom Finney in his overcoat - there would have been four men marking him when we were kickin' in"

"When I´ve got nothing better to do, I look down the league table to see how Everton are getting along"

"The trouble with referees is that they know the rules, but they don't know the game"

"A football team is like a piano. You need eight men to carry it and three who can play the damn thing"

"The difference between Everton and the Queen Mary is that Everton carry more passengers!"

"At a football club, there's a holy trinity – the players, the manager and the supporters. Directors don't come into it. They are only there to sign the cheques"

"First is first and second is nowhere"

Bixente Lizarazu

"If we don't know what to do with the ball, we always give it to Zidane! He can always handle it"

"He (Patrice Evra) blames us for dirtying his image but he is doing a great job of it himself"

"Spain's play is like love without the sex. It lacks a bit of spice"

Bobby Charlton

"It was a fair decision, the penalty, even it was inside or outside the box"

"Some people tell me that we professional players are soccer slaves. Well, if this is slavery, give me a life sentence"

"They know on the Continent that European football without the English is like a hot dog without the mustard"

Bobby Gould

"Football these days isn't going forwards. It's going sidewards"

"They're being asked to play three games a week - mentally, they can't ascertain to do that"

Bobby Moore

"If you never concede a goal, you're going to win more games than you lose"

Bobby Robson

"The first ninety minutes of a football match are the most important"

"We didn´t underestimate them. They were just a lot better than we thought"

"I would have given my right arm to be a pianist"

"I´ve had to come out of the dressing room because I don´t want to get too excited"

He never fails to hit the target. But that was a miss"

"Anything from 1-0 to 2-0 would be a nice result"

"We´re taking 22 players to Italy, sorry, to Spain where are we, Jim?"

"Players never know why they are taken off or substituted - until they become managers"

"The margin is very marginal"

Bob Paisley

"If you`re in the penalty area and don´t know what to do with the ball, put it in the net and we´ll discuss the options later"

"Still we've had the hard times too - one year we finished second"

"Its not about the long ball or the short ball, its about the right ball"

Bob Wilson

"Diego Maradona… a flawed genius who has now become a genius who is flawed"

Brad Friedel

"When you sign a contract to play football professionally, part of that agreement should be an undertaking to be a positive role model"

"For a goalkeeper, there is no hiding place"

"A great goalkeeper has to have the keys to a great mindset. To be able to work well in the box, I believe you have to be able to think outside the box"

"I'll make continuous and instantaneous risk assessments about the action I should take in relation to the flight of a spheroid object. That's what my job is really all about"

"My colleagues spend most of their time with their backs turned towards me"

Branko Brnovic

"This team (Montenegro) can be a match for anyone"

Brendan Rodgers

"It's not always plain sailing , especially when you're flying"

"You train dogs, I like to educate players"

Bret Holman

"You always think you're going to get one of those chances in the game and you actually finally do and it doesn't go in the back of the net"

"I'm not the prettiest footballer, I'm not there to score the scissor kicks and do the back-heels"

Brian Clough

"It only takes a second to score a goal"

"They say Rome wasn´t built in a day, but I wasn´t on that particular job"

"I wouldn´t say I was the best manager in the business. But I was in the top one"

"If I had an argument with a player we would sit down for twenty minutes, talk about it and then decide I was right!"

"Players lose you games, not tactics. There's so much crap talked about tactics by people who barely know how to win at dominoes"

"Acne is a bigger problem than injuries"

"Arsenal caresses a football the way I dreamed of caressing Marilyn Monroe"

"At last England have appointed a manager (Sven Göran Eriksson) who speaks English better than the players"

"Players lose you games, not tactics. There's so much crap talked about tactics by people who barely know how to win at dominoes"

"Dutch goalkeepers are protected to a ridiculous extent. The only time they're in danger of physical contact is when they go into a red light district"

Brian Greenhoff

"All the team are 100% behind the manager, but I can't speak for the rest of the squad"

Brian Horton

"It was a game of two halves and we were rubbish in both of them"

Brian Laudrup

"He (Paul Gascoigne) is a fantastic player - when he isn't drunk"

Bruce Arena

"Let's face it, they never like the ball (goalkeepers). The only time they would be happy is if it was square and heavy"

Bruce Grobbellar

"That's a question mark everyone's asking"

"If you can stay alive and enjoy life, that's the whole heart and soul of life. That's why I played with a smile on my face all these years"

"Life is too short to sit around doing nothing"

Bryan Robson

"If we played like this every week, we wouldn't be so inconsistent"

Cameron Hepple

"I didn't have confirmed aspirations of becoming a professional footballer until I was about 13. I always dream´t about it, but growing up in the Bahamas we did not have the professional footballer culture, we just played for fun and I guess parents just wanted their kids to do something to stay active"

Carles Rexach

"To play football you should not suffer. With suffering you can not succeed"

Carlo Ancelotti

"Had we scored, the tie would look very different now"

"I'm going to put two mastiffs on him (Andrea Pirlo)"

"If he (Mourinho) thinks he is Jesus, I am certainly not one of his apostles!"

Carlos Alberto

"Football is something that gets under your skin and never leaves you"

"Choose one and hit hard"

Carlos Ruiz

"You show people what you're like as a player when you're out on the field. You show people what you're like as a person the rest of the time"

Carlos Sanchez

"I didn't know very much about Judo before Wednesday night. Now I know a little more about it. Pepe almost took my arm off!"

Carlos Tevez

"But let me tell you I am not enjoying the life of a footballer"

"After the game you can not do anything"

Carlos Timoteo Griguol

"Buy yourself the department before the car"

Carlos Valderrama

"I think that during my sporting career I already did what I enjoy most in life - playing football"

"The game is over. There are no more Valderrama. The coaches make them disappear. They do not want any more players with that quality"

"I was long enough in training camps. They always killed me"

Cesc Fàbregas

"I really like playing football on my Xbox in my boxer shorts"

Celso Borges

"I'll try not to disappoint anyone"

"Whats most difficult is to adapt to the new country"

Cesare Maldini

"When you score one goal more than the other team in a cup tie it is always enough"

César Delgado

"The baguette. It's amazing how good it is, the baguette"

César Luis Menotti

"Our football belongs to the working class and has the size, nobility and generosity to allow everyone to enjoy it as a spectacle"

"I would like to congratulate Claudio Coutinho on his moral victory. I hope he will congratulate me on the real one"

"The Italians not defend well, it´s defending with many"

Cha Du-Ri

"Freddie Ljungberg is a very famous player and I like his underwear. I have a lot of Calvin Klein underwear at home, maybe I'll show him"

Chan Wai Ho

"Just playing well in yourself is not enough"

Charles Ntamark

"It may be that I am marking Maradona in the opening match. We know all about him, but he doesn't know anything about me"

Charlie Nicholas

"Scottish football needs a kick in the arm"

Cheik Tiote

"We have great players so we have to win something. We have to win this Cup of Nations. Every time there is an African tournament people tell us that we are favourites to win. But when you look at our trophy cabinet there is nothing there. Absolutely nothing"

Chris Coleman

"Football is like fighting a gorilla – you don't stop when you're tired, you can only stop when the gorilla is tired"

Chris Jones

"The new West Stand casts a giant shadow over the entire pitch, even on a sunny day"

Chris Kamara

"It's real end-to-end stuff... but unfortunately it's all up at Forest's end"

"Is it still called Calcutta? I thought it was Bombay these days"

Chris Powell

"I am going to say to Yann (Kermorgant) that all 23 other teams are called Leicester City"

Chris Turner

"I've told the players we need to win so that I can have the cash to buy some new ones"

Chris Waddle

"There's going to be four or five teams battling for the top six spots"

"That was a great finish, but you could say it wasn't a great finish because it didn't go in"

"The 2,000 away fans will be unhappy. In fact half of them have gone, there's only 500 left "

Christer Yussef

"I am an offensive midfielder with good speed - which is my best feature"

Christian Vieri

"This is the latest invention that you have invented"

Christian Ziege

"I am the left, more middle, defensive oriented, offensive player"

Christiano Ronaldo

"Your love makes me strong, your hate makes me unstoppable"

"Some fans keep booing and whistling at me because I'm handsome, rich and a great player - they envy me"

"I'm living a dream I never want to wake up from"

"Being too humble isn't good. In Portugal, we say 'Too much humility is vanity'"

"If I am named the best in the world, it won't be a surprise to me"

Christoph Daum

"You don't always need to have an absolute majority behind you, sometimes 51 percent is enough"

Clarke Carlisle

"It's an unprecedented precedent"

"Andros Townsend gave it to his full back, turned and opened up his legs"

"It's an unprecedented precedent"

Claude Le Roy

"Football is a permanent orgasm"

Claudio Caniggia

"River is the better school. They demand attractive football. Boca is different. There the fans keep cheering even when you're losing"

Cláudio Coutinho

"We are the moral champions (WC 1978)"

Claudio Gentile

"Football is not for ballerinas"

Claudio Ranieri

"Being a coach in Italy is like being a skydiver who doesn't know if his parachute is going to open"

"Hello my sharks (Media), welcome to the funeral"

Claudio Taffarel

"We were apathetic in game when we couldn't be apathetic - We just didn't play well"

"The truth is that I was passionate about staying involved in football, but I didn't have the patience to be a coach"

Clayton Blackmore

"It's never over until somebody sings"

”You certainly knew where you stood with the boss (Alex Ferguson)”

Climax Lawrence

”Consistency has been our hallmark”

Clint Dempsey

”Important thing for a player is to make sure that's you're playing. You're playing well and playing consistently”

Clyde Best

”The most important thing to remember is the that ball doesn't care what color you are”

”With all of the foolishness that is going on with the racism and stuff like that, the minute a goal is scored, I can be as black as the ace of spades or I can be as white as a snow flake - the minute a goal is scored, everybody hugs one another”

"People weren't used to seeing people of color on the field in those days. I was always taught that you're not playing for yourself, you're playing for the people who are coming behind you, and that's what kept me going"

Co Adriaanse

"Most tall players are technically weak, that's because their brains are so far away from their feet"

Cobi N’Gai Jones

”I never thought I’d play soccer past high school, so to go from that team to actually being most-capped and three World” Cups is pretty special”

Coco Basile

"I perfectly place the players on the field. When the game begins they move"

Craig Brown

"He's (Michael Owen) got the legs of a salmon"

Cristian Ramírez

"I'll go one step at a time"

DaMarcus Beasley

"When I got here, people would do the monkey noises and chants and stuff like that. I just kind of laugh it off"

Dadá Maravilha

"There are only three great powers in the universe: God in heaven, the pope in the Vatican and Dadá in the great box"

"My shooting technique is so poor that if someday I score from outside the box, the keeper has to be banned from football"

"There is no such thing as an ugly goal. Ugly is not to score a goal"

"I was so focused in scoring goals that I didn't have time to learn how to play football"

Damiano Tommasi

"We want to be an example"

Daniel Alves

"Manchester City have no class, they've bought success"

Daniel Davari

"Politics should not play a role in sports"

"You have to make your own luck"

Daniel Passarella

"I ask faith and trust"

Daniel Van Buyten

"I can't burn the candle at both ends now I'm nearly 36"

"You never stop learning"

"If I think back to where I come from, the small village of Froidchapelle. I started with the bottom team in the lowest league. You couldn't be any lower. I really was at the bottom"

Daniele De Rossi

"The nickname Capitano Futuro is now becoming a sentence. I'll have to wear the vice-captain armband forever!"

Danny Blanchflower

"(Duchess of Kent asked why the Leicester City players had names on their tracksuits and the Tottenham team didn´t) "Well, you see we all know each other!"

"I asked the manager for a ball to train with. He couldn´t have looked more horrified if I´d asked for a transfer. He told me they never used a ball at Barnsley. The theory was that we´d be hungry for it on Saturday if we didn´t see it for the rest of the week. I told him that Saturday I probably wouldn't recognise it"

"Winning isn't everything, but wanting to win is"

"It´s our new tactic - we equalise before the others have scored"

Darijo Srna

"I am very grateful for all that I have achieved in my lifetime"

"For me, it is incredible that there are children in this world who have to grow up without parents. I want them just a little help"

Darío Sala

"My wife didn´t know anything about soccer when we started dating. Worst of all – had never heard of Diego Maradona"

Dave Bassett

"An inch or two either side of the post and that would have been a goal"

"If the goalkeeper wasn't there, it would've been a goal"

Dave Beasant

"His (Dave Basset) mouth sometimes loses contact with his brains"

Dave Whelan

"Roberto Martinez's belief is unbelievable"

David Beckham

"I only have to open my mouth and I get totally slaughtered"

"I definitely want Brooklyn to be christened, but I don't know into what religion yet"

"My parents have been there for me, ever since I was about 7"

"Alex Ferguson is the best manager I've ever had at this level. Well, he's the only manager I've actually had at this level. But he's the best manager I've ever had"

"I didn't see him (Pele) live obviously, because I wasn't born"

"My new tattoo is Jesus being carried by three cherubs. Obviously the cherubs are my boys"

"I would walk back from the United States to play for England again"

"That was in the past - we´re in the future now."

"There´s no one to blaim – the´re just individual mistakes"

David Craig

"The problem is nobody knows what the problem is"

David Ginola

"There are some great defenders here, I just don't know their names"

"Football is a matter of creativity and imagination"

David Luiz

"People sometimes ask 'why are you so happy?' and I reply 'why aren't you?'"

David Moyes

"I remember my first game against Fulham – I remember it like it was tomorrow"

"I've just seen the replay again for the first time"

David Obua

"You have to go out there and fight every day"

David Pleat

"A game is not won until it is lost"

"This is a real cat and carrot situation"

"I feel sorry for Wolves at the moment but not sorry for them"

"In the last year, 46 of the 92 managers have lost their jobs – that's over half"

David Suazo

"It's hard to be a fan"

"Football generates a lot of emotions and is very rewarding"

David Trezeguet

"I want to make something bright in this cup , but I see the same determination in others"

Davor Šuker

"I consider myself as a small ambassador of Real Madrid out of Spain"

Dean Holdsworth

"The only way we will be going to Europe is if the club splash out and take us all to Eurodisney"

Dejan Stefanovic

"We (Portsmouth) have lots of foreign players at the moment. They are all good players but we need more British players with a British mentality for the Premiership. We need that fighting spirit"

Demba Ba

"Often you can close your eyes, hit and score. Sometimes you try every trick in the book but the ball refuses to go in"

Demba Savage

”It is always difficult to play against a team that is in the league table bottom, and fighting for the survival”

Denis Law

”The only thing that has never changed in the history of the game is the shape of the ball”

”It was one of those goals that's invariably a goal”

”I lost count of the times he let me down”

”He was one of the best inside-forwards of his or any other generation”

”Who ever wins today will win the championship, no matter who wins”

Dennis Bergkamp

"Behind every kick of the ball there has to be a thought"

Désiré Mbonabucya

”People now finally know how to pronounce my name"

Dickson Ehutu

”I went to Chelsea dressingroom to swap shirts and it was bigger than my house!”

Didi

"Training is training, the game is the game"

Didier Deschamps

“I'm not going to go fishing for whales if all I'm going to catch is sardines”

Didier Drogba

"Our number one opponents are not Liverpool, Arsenal or Manchester United. It is ourselves at Chelsea"

"I want to make clear that I don't dive"

"In football you can't stay up all the time"

Diego Forlan

"Every coach has his own players. Maybe I was not the player that Sir Alex (Ferguson) liked, which is fair enough. He can choose - that's why he's the manager"

Diego Maradona

"The goal was scored a little bit by the hand of God, another bit by the head of Maradona"

"The problem is that they are all stars at Madrid. You need someone to carry the water to the well"

"Best? My mother says it was me and Pele's mother says it was him"

"God makes me play well. That is why I always make the sign of the cross when I walk out onto the pitch. I feel I would be betraying him if I didn't"

"Lionel Messi scores a goal and celebrates. Cristiano scores a goal and poses like he's in a shampoo commercial"

Diego Simeone

"When I saw him (Diego Costa) in training, I wanted to die"

"What happens on the field stays on the field"

Dietmar Hamann

"The FA inquiry has been a farce from start to finish and it's not even finished"

Dimitar Berbatov

"For the most important thing is to entertain"

"Football is like art and my aim is to create beautiful things on the pitch"

Dimitar Penev

"Football is a simple game for simple people, but you are supposed to play it intelligently"

Dimitris Salpingidis

"I see the ball, my opponent's position and I don't blink - I just shoot to score"

Dino Zoff

"To Gazza (Paul Gascoigne), ice cream is more important than his credit cards"

Dirceu

"I would pass them a ball, and they'd return me a watermelon"

Djamel Zidane

"The level of African teams are far from the same level to allow them to compete with the big teams who play the title"

Dunga

"I like to see exquisite football, but it not gives the title"

"We know world-class players are always outstanding at any time"

"Calling me a donkey doesn't offend me because they are one of the most hard-working animals"

Dwight Yorke

"They're a little bit miss and hit"

"The game is not over until it is"

"He (Roy Keane) warned players he would not settle for anyone taking their foot off the pedal. It was leadership by inspiring fear"

Eamon Dunphy

"You need dictatorships and poverty to produce great footballers"

"They've (Barcelona) given us memories that we will never forget, and we should remember that"

"Machiavelli was an Italian... Wasn't he, John? Who did he play for?"

Ebbe Skovdahl

"Statistics are like miniskirts - They give you good ideas but hide the important things"

Eddy Etaeta

"We have guys (Tahiti national team) doing different jobs, but nine of the squad are unemployed. Some of them are delivery boys, a truck driver, some of them are PE teachers, some are accountants"

Edin Džeko

"I am too good to spend another season on the bench"

"I have never given up anything in my life"

"No one will forget that day (ManU-City 1-6), even United fans"

Edinson Cavani

"The winner always finds the solution. The looser always finds an excuse"

Eidur Gudjohnsen

"Whenever I get an opportunity I'm determined to take advantage and know I have to do that"

El Hadji Diouf

"You can hate me, but you can love my football"

"I do not honestly know what is really happening in Libya at the moment but it must be very hard for Gaddafi and his family"

Elías Figueroa

"The box is my house - I decide who let in!"

Emanuel Amunike

"Making people happy, making them smile - it doesn't get any better than that for a footballer."

"The most difficult part of being a footballer is when you can't fight back. Not being able to play because your body won't respond to what you're telling it is the worst thing"

Emerson Leão

"We enter to win, not to compete"

Emile Heskey

"You can never say never, unless you say never yourself"

Emmanuel Adebayor

"My country is my country and I'm going to play for them whether they like it or not"

"The coach was not a help me, I was on the pitch, so I couldn't do both jobs (coaching and playing)"

"It´s like (AC Milan was after him) a boy being told Beyoncé is looking for him"

"Players don't feel comfortable with (Francesco) Guidolin. He speaks in Italian and we understand nothing"

Emmanuel Petit

"I wish people could live on the Moon so we could send all the crazy people there"

"Winning the World Cup is the most beautiful thing to have happened to France since the Revolution"

Emmanuel Scheffer

"As now we have three training. - The players wanted to know on which days - I replied - At 7 o´clock, at 11 o´clock and at 15 o´clock"

Enis Alushi

"In the end it is our job to make our dreams alive"

Eoin Hand

"There are only two certainties in life. People die, and football managers get the sack"

Éric Cantona

"My best moment? I have a lot of good moments but the one I prefer is when I kicked the hooligan"

"When the seagulls follow the trawler, it is because they think sardines will be thrown into the sea"

"It is fortunate that most players are not like me or there would be anarchy"

"You are constantly battling against your own weaknesses yo make a good performance"

"Anyone who is different or is slightly out of the norm, is considered crazy"

"An artist is someone with the gift to light up a dark room"

"When people are talking about you, it means that you exist"

"I am searching for abstract ways of expressing reality, abstract forms that will enlighten my own mystery"

"I am mistrustful of people who are constantly over-intellectualizing things. It kills passion. You have to allow yourself to lose control from time to time"

"I didn't study; I live"

"I prefer to play and lose than win, because I know in advance I'm going to win"

"I stopped playing football because I'd done as much as I could. I needed something which was going to excite me as much as football has excited me"

"Sometimes in life one experiences an emotion which is so strong that it is difficult to think, or to reason"

"I'm proud of what I achieved there, but life on memories is not much of a life"

"It is enjoyable to make things visible which are invisible"

"Often there are players who have only football as a way of expressing themselves and never develop other interest. And when they no longer play football, they no longer do anything; they no longer exist, or rather they have the sensation of no longer existing"

"Socrates worked towards making people question themselves. He like to provoke self-interrogation but wasn't particularly interested in the answers that emerged; he just like to set off the thought process"

"I try to find different ways of expressing myself. Without that I will die"

"Sometimes you get submerged by emotion. I think it's very important to express it - which doesn't necessarily mean hitting someone"

"I am not a man. I am Cantona!"

Éric Deflandre

I take my soccer boots and an inflatable doll because a month (EURO-2000) without a woman will be difficult"

Ernst Happel

"A day without football is a day lost"

"If you mark man-to-man, you're sending out eleven donkeys"

"Fear isn't in my vocabulary"

"If you really examine your own opinions, you'll normally come up with a better one"

Esteban Cambiasso

"Losing the final hurts my soul"

Ethan Zohn

"If I can make an impact, I want to help some kids and bridge the gap between soccer and celebrity in America"

Eusébio

"Although football is a sport, but it represents more"

"I always had both feet firmly on the ground"

"Anyone can play whether you are poor or rich. All you need is space and a ball"

Fabian Lustenberger

"It's a nice thing (after winning 6-1) for the fans. If we get stuffed 6-0 next week nobody will care any more"

Fabio Capello

"If you want to score a goal, you have to hit the target"

"Serie A is wonderful. Serie B is depressing. And you have to be on drugs to watch Serie C"

"I know about Feyenoord, is that they are from the country of Ajax"

Fabrizio Ravanelli

"In my little boys head, I never said english players are overweight, knackered and drunk"

Fan Zhiyi

"I hated retiring as a player because I love playing the game and I will never quit football"

Ferenc Puskas

"Il will write my life as a footballer as if it were a love story, for who shall say it is not? It began with my great love of football and it will end the same way"

"We're going to be all right, they've got someone even smaller than me"

"You can only kick with one foot at a time, otherwise you fall on your ass"

Fernando Santos

"Everyone has to respect Greeks because of its history and the principles of democracy, science... everything started from Greece, so it's very difficult for anyone to give us lessons"

Fernando Torres

"Sometimes I'd like to have a conversation with a friend in a restaurant without feeling I'm being watched. At this rate I will have to go on holiday to Greenland"

Filippo Inzaghi

"The key was our heart, determination. At one moment we thought we were out. Then I had some good luck on that rebound from the post"

"My presence keeps the linesmen extremely busy for the whole 90 minutes"

Francesco Totti

"My dream? To have a third child and to win the Champions League. The only major trophy I have not won"

Francisco Gento

"Puskas left foot was so good that he could even juggle the soap in the showers"

Francisco Maturana García

"Every defeat is a victory in itself"

Francisco Rojas

"Journalists always come up with things that are never lies"

Francisco Varallo

"However, in my whole life I've never felt such a bitter pain as losing that World Cup Final against Uruguay in 1930"

Frank Farina

"We've got a monster around our neck after beating England, but we must feed it"

Franck Ribéry

"I told Pep (Guardiola), this is a goal for you, against Mourinho"

Frank Rijkaard

"In football you cannot afford to get overwhelmed by euphoria or sadness, it is important to stay on an even keel"

Franz Beckenbauer

"We used to get our old players coming to watch training with football magazines in their hands. Now, more often than not, they´re checking their share prices"

"You know the Dutch, they're always a bit funny - some of them"

"They (Bayern players) are all like prostitutes. They smoke, they´re lazy and they sleep all day"

"If you put all the German players, except Kahn, in a sack and hit it, you would get someone who deserved it"

"Practice doesn't make perfect, perfect practice makes perfect"

"Players complain about playing too many games, but one year I played 15 months of football"

"One can win each game, one can also lose each game"

Freddie Ljungberg

"These rumours (that I´m gay) are completely false. I've only watched two musicals during my entire spell in London and they are Mamma Mia and Saturday Night Fever"

Frederic Kanoute

"I don't really like the north. It's always raining, it's really cold and I don't like all those little houses"

"When people in England see the goals I'm scoring in Spain, they must think I have a really good twin brother!"

Gabriel Agbonlahor

"I don't pick them (Nike boots), they're a bit dodgy but we have to wear them"

Gabriel Batistuta

"To be honest, I couldn't care less what the others think"

Gabriel Boştină

"I don't know how many goals we need to eliminate Betis - as many would be sufficient"

Gabriel Cichero

"There is nothing compared to being able to bring together 30 million people"

Gabriel Tamas

"I think that if we would have scored more goals than them we would have won"

Gabriel Torres

"I first dedicate my goals to God and I like to dance as well as dedicate them to my daughter"

Gaël Clichy

"If you end up at Man City, I really believe you are a player who thinks only about money"

Garrincha

"If I shoot with both my feet I´ll fall on the ground"

Gennaro Gattuso

"Some German newspapers criticized us. Mainly they offended our country, when they spoke of spaghetti and mafia to describe us. Hopefully their women know the Italians"

"Pirlo has the face of an angel, but he is a son of a bitch! He´s always making jokes, always breaking the rules. One time when I was eating at Milanello, I had the bright idea of leaving my phone on the table, and he sent a text message from it to Galliani and Braida offering them my sister!"

"I'm no Brad Pitt, but there's worse out there than me"

"Even if Marcello Lippi decided to send me home I would have chained myself to the team bus. You would have had to call the police to take me away"

"Either you do things seriously or you don't do them at all"

Garry Birtles

"They were numerically outnumbered"

Garth Crooks

"Mistakes will be made, make no mistake"

"Football's football. If that weren't the case, it wouldn't be the game that it is"

Gary Lineker

"There's no in between you're either good or bad - We were in between"

"Football is a simple game. 22 men chase a ball for 90 minutes and at the end, the Germans win"

"Footballers are more likely to work better if they get a pat on the back from the boss. A knife in the back is never the answer"

"Wrighty (Ian Wright), are you a fan of S&M (Serbia & Montenegro)?"

Gary McSheffrey

"It was wonderful to get on for my debyt - next time it would be relly nice if I could touch the ball"

Gary Medel

"For my own sake, it's a good job that I chose football. If not, perhaps I'd be stealing or drug-trafficking"

Gary Neville

"Before games, the smell of burgers wafts down from the stands"

"This is the real thing, this is no pony show"

"The rest of the Spice Girls wanted to invite the entire Bayern Munich team because they reckoned they'd never known blokes to be on top for 90 minutes and still come second"

George Best

"I spent a lot of money on booze, birds and fast cars. The rest I just squandered"

"I used to go missing a lot - Miss Canada, Miss United Kingdom, Miss World"

"Pain is temporary, glory lasts forever!"

"In 1969 I gave up women and alcohol... it was the worst 20 minutes of my life"

"I might go to Alcoholics Anonymous, but I think it would be difficult for me – to be anonymous"

"They'll forget all the rubbish when I've gone and they'll remember the football. If only one person thinks I'm the best player in the world, that's good enough for me"

George Graham

"Wayne Rooney really has a man's body on a teenager's head"

George Weah

"Once you take care of people, people respect you"

"I will do nothing for 89 minutes, but score in the 90th"

"I am a peaceful man. No matter what they say"

"It can't be Sunday every day. There are also Mondays and Tuesdays"

Georgi Kinkladze

"All the players want to win and the goals will follow"

Georgi Kondratiev

"It could have been better, it could have been worse"

Georgios Samaras

"When you're psychologically high, you're feeling good about yourself and feeling positive. That's a totally different thing from your mentality"

"If you play at an English Premier League club, finishing 11th or 12th, the only thing you will remember when you retire is the money"

Gerard Houllier

"You can't say my team aren't winners. They've proved that by finishing fourth, third and second in the last three years"

"There are those who say maybe I should forget about football. Maybe I should forget about breathing"

Gerard Piqué

"Sometimes we may seem untouchable, oblivious to everything but it's not true … one day I would like to invite someone to visit the locker room and he would be surprised... Well, there is a guy who hunts for mushrooms, another visits Warner Park with friends on his day off, another goes to a restaurant to have dinner for 20 euros so he can go with all his crew"

Gerd Müller

"God help them (goalkeepers). Often I didn't know where the ball was going, so how could they"

"He´s (Messi) only defect is that he doesn't play for Bayern Munich"

Gernot Rohr

"My first Nations Cup, it's a beautiful adventure. It's like the first time with a woman, it makes your heart beat faster. It's nice to experience that at my age!"

Gerry Birtles

"When I was having my long goalless run, people told me that if I´d shot John Lennon he´d still be alive today"

Gerry Francis

"What I said to them at half-time would be unprintable on radio"

Getaneh Kebede

"That is life as this injuries can happen to any players. I however gave the team moral support"

Gheorghe Hagi

"Kids, go to school! It's good for something..."

Giancarlo Maldonado

"I have the willingness to take commitment"

Gianfranco Zola

"Ninety-five per cent of my language problems are the fault of that stupid little midget (Dennis Wise)"

Gianluca Vialli

"When Manchester United are at their best I am close to orgasm"

"Well, as the saying goes, football is an old, funny game"

"It's only a game but it's life and death to me"

Gianluigi Buffon

"I would say that I am having less sex now that I'm playing in Serie B – there is more to think about in this division"

"You score goals as a kid. Then you grow up stupid and become a goalkeeper"

Gianni Rivera

"I'm a happy man because my hobby and my profession are one and the same"

Giles De Bilde

"My only happiness at Sheffield Wednesday was the state of my bank account"

Giorgos Karagounis

"I can say that we managed to overcome huge obstacles. When we left Greece, we all said in one voice, 'We will give everything'"

"We have nothing to prove to anyone"

Giovanni Trapattoni

"There is only one ball. And if the opponent has it, you have to ask yourself – why?"

"We can't behave like crocodiles and cry over spilled milk and broken eggs"

"Managers are like fish, after a while they start to smell"

Giuseppe Meazza

"Luckily I lived near the stadium, and I managed to get there in a rush. My teammates and the coach looked at me disapprovingly. It was only five minutes before the kick-off, so I quickly changed and joined the team on the pitch. I could hear the Inter directors saying: 'We'll deal with him after the match. We'll find out what he's been up to.' Luckily I scored a hat-trick so afterward no one said a word!"

Glenn Hoddle

"He is a goal scorer not a natural born one - not yet. That takes time"

"When a player gets to 30, so does his body"

"There's a lot of work been put in that hasn't been put in"

"Getting picked gives you half that confidence, or 50% of it"

Guus Hiddink

"I never can predict my future because a big part of the future is already behind me"

Gokotu Sakai

"I've only been here in Germany for a few days but what I have noticed is that people drink beer even in the afternoon"

Gordon Banks

"Goal is like a knife in the ribs"

Gordon McQueen

"Ask all the players in the country which club they would like to play for and 99% would say 'Manchester United'. The other 1% are lier's"

Gordon Strachan

"It´s an incredible rise to stardom (Wayne Rooney). At 17 you´re more likely to get a call from Michael Jackson than Sven Goran Eriksson"

"The world looks a totally different place after two wins"

"He could have done one of three things. He didn't do either"

"If you can manage Celtic, you can be Prime Minister"

Graeme Le Saux

"The opening ceremony was good, although I missed it"

"Santi Cazorla is two-footed"

"Ramires is involved in everything he does"

"We're in a no-win situation, except if we win we'll go through to the next round"

Graeme Souness

"He's not the best of players (Gennaro Gattuso). He's a little dog. He'll scuttle around but he's well past his sell-buy date"

"I think if you want to win the title you'll have to finish above both these teams"

"It's like a stone rolling down a hill - it's gathering more and more moss"

Graham Roberts

"Football is a game of skill, we kicked them a bit and they kicked us a bit"

Graham Taylor

"I was just saying to your colleague, the referee has got me the sack, thank him ever so much for that, won´t you?"

Graig Johnston

"Playing soccer for Australia would be like surfing for England"

Grzegorz Lato

"Often Then asking me if I would like something in life refurnish. No. Nothing"

Günther Netzer

"For me, heading a ball was similar to touching the ball with your hands"

Gustavo Poyet

"I'd go back to Leeds at any time, but not right now"

"I understand the game one way - the game is played with one football, so you need to use it"

Hans Mayer

"Nobody loves me, you can ask my wife"

Hao Haidong

"It might sound cliched that a talented player must also work hard, but to achieve greater success you need to put in more effort"

Harald Brattbakk

"I always loved football, but I never really believed that I could make a career of it"

Harry Kewell

"I've always been a childhood Liverpool fan, even when I was a kid"

Harry Redknapp

"John Hartson's got more previous than Jack the Ripper"

"I've seen better fights at a wedding"

Harouna Doula

"I obey my bosses and accept their decisions, all for the sake of a functioning team"

Helenio Herrera

"We won without getting off the bus"

Henri Saivet

"You've got to have several bows to your string"

Hernan Crespo

"I just do not like how the Germans celebrated the victory over us. Jumping at every corner of the stadium"

"I grew up with Diego he was my idol. But I also played with Messi. Maradona or Messi? You can never forget history, but I´d say Messi"

"I thought at the time it was a beautiful goal, now I want to go and watch it on the TV to see how magical it really was"

"I earn £82,000 a week and work three hours a day but life's hard when you can't read the electricity bill"

Hernanes

"I couldn't actually write with my toes. But I tried. And it helped"

Hernan Medford

"In soccer anything can happen"

"I'm a very direct person who likes to get to the point"

Herve Renard

"(Jonas) Sakuwaha is more important than Zambia? Me, I don't care about the name of the player. The player has to show me what he can do and the determination"

Hiroshi Nanami

"I learned about the subtleties of positioning from Vanenburg and Dunga always gave exactly the right instructions for the situation. I learned so much from them"

Hossam Hassan

"Football is the core of my life and I just cannot stop thinking about it"

Howard Kendall

"I made a number of enquiries and everyone said the same thing: He´s (Eric Cantona) totally unsuitable for English football. Needless to say, I acted on that information and turned him down"

Howard Wilkinson

"I'm a firm believer that if the other side scores first you have to score twice to win"

"If they hadn't scored, we would've won"

"There´s only two types of manager. Those who´ve been sacked and those who will be sacked in then future"

Hristo Stoichkov

"If you understand football, you make substitutions during the match, if you don't you make comments after it"

"Soccer is simple. You just need to have the right mentality, fighting in every game, in every practice and for every ball"

"If Bale is worth €100million, I would have been priceless. No Englishman who has ever come to Spanish football has succeeded"

"Now I know for sure that God is Bulgarian (WC 1994)"

"God is still Bulgarian but the referee was French (After losing to Italy WC 1994)"

Hugo Sanchez

"Whoever invented football should be worshiped as a God"

Hussain Al-Hadhri

"In Arabic there is a saying that translates roughly as: 'If you have two things in mind you only lie to yourself'"

Iain Dowie

"It's now much more fifty-fifty in favor of Everton"

"Belgium are outside dark favorites to win the group"

Ian Holloway

"As long as you hit the target, they're going to go in - if the keeper don't make a save"

"Some weeks the lady is good looking and some weeks she's not. Our performance today would not have been the best looking bird but at least we got her in the taxi"

"In the first-half we were like the Dog and Duck, in the second-half we were like Real Madrid. We can't go on like that. At full-time I was at them like an irritated Jack Russell"

"I watched Hamlet the other night and, what a shame, they nearly all died in the end. I've never heard so many words make so little sense. It was brilliant, a bit like my interviews"

"I love Blackpool. We're very similar. We both look better in the dark"

Ian McNail

"We actually got the winner three minutes from the end but then they equalized"

Ian Rush

"I couldn't settle in Italy. It was like living in a foreign country"

"It's best being a striker. If you miss five, then score the winner, you're a hero. The goalkeeper can play a blinder, then let one in, and he's a villain"

Ian St John

"Batistuta gets most of his goals with the ball"

Ian Wright

"Without being too harsh on David Beckham, he cost us the match"

"He (Edgar Davids) looks like a dread-locked tea pot!"

"I don't want Rooney to leave these shores but if he does, I think he'll go abroad"

"If Bergkamp were in 'Star Trek', he'd be the best player in solar system"

"I was once fined £5,000 for calling Coventry fans wankers. Best £5,000 I ever spent"

"The ref was booking so many I thought he was filling his lotto numbers"

Ibrahima Traoré

"As many know, sometimes in football, there are choices to make. There are people who do not understand this"

"I want to be the best African player and the best player of Guinea. This is not arrogance. I say this because I think I have the capacity"

Igor Štimac

"Some of our younger players gave up football completely to go off and fight for Croatia. It was felt that the top players, the internationals, had a duty to carry on. When we played for Croatia, we were letting the rest of the world know that Croatia existed"

Igoris Pankratjevas

"You still have to prove everything on the pitch"

Iker Casillas

"It's not about advantages, it is about how you perform on the night"

"I don't want to be remembered as a good goalkeeper, I want to be remembered as a great person"

Islam Slimani

"I´m extreme lazy during the month of Ramadhan, I exceed the limits. It is very difficult to me me"

"The dishes made by my mom are the best in the world"

Ivan Zamorano

"When I go to Madrid, my son always asks me for a shirt, but with the 10 of Messi, his idol. There´s something wrong in his head"

James Clarkson

"I feel cheated. The person who came up with these rules must be a candidate for a madhouse (after strange game Barbados 4–2 Grenada). The game should never be played with so many players running around the field confused. Our players did not even know which direction to attack: our goal or their goal. I have never seen this happen before. In football, you are supposed to score against the opponents to win, not for them"

James Rodríguez

"It makes me proud when they compare me to great players. But I am James and I continue to be James. I am my own person and the world can see me that way"

Jamie Redknapp

"Most goals are scored between the posts"

"Will Chelsea qualify with ease? I think they will, but it won't be easy"

Jan Mølby

"We had a belief that we believed in"

Jan Åge Fjørtoft

"Jorg Berger is such a good coach, he had even saved the Titanic"

Jason McAteer

"What is your position at the company (Credit card application) - Right back"

"Jordan Henderson is a player who likes to do his business in the middle of the park"

"We seem to be a side that if we don't score we get beat"

Javad Nekounam

"I really enjoy scoring goals"

"Life here (Osasuna) is very different from Iran"

"I don't appreciate their (North Korea) style of play"

Javier Clemente

"This is an unusual Scotland side because they have good players"

Javier Hernández

"You can't be a good player without your teammates"

"I am very eager to play as my club don't take me much into account"

"I lost all confidence in myself and I questioned whether that was the path what God had chosen for me"

Javier Zanetti

"I keep my hair in order. Also in the field. Also under a thunderstorm. Even if I run in the middle of the gusts of wind. Everyone my team-mates and even my wife, ask me how do I finish the game always combed"

Jeff Strasser

"Good things come to those who wait"

Jean-Marie Pfaff

"I do not need attention. I'm familiar enough. What I do, I like it. If I can make people a favor or help, please. But personally I do not have to be. In the spotlight I have all the blablabla and attention needed"

"Not everyone can stand there in the middle of a big goal and face up to all those big guys bearing down on you"

Jeff Agoos

"I'm not one to rank memories in order of importance. They're all special in their own way"

Jens Lehmann

"You don't feel sorry for yourself, you get on with life"

"If I have a lot of adrenaline in my body, that is helpful because I feel less pain"

"Goalkeeping is like extreme sports sometimes – you have to let yourself go"

Jérémy Ménez

"Running is for the others. I'm here for the attacking play."

Jerry Bengtson

"What I do, I know why I do it"

"I love goals, I enjoy them very much but I don't like to celebrate them with euphoria, I don't and I can't change that"

Jim Leighton

"If I went upfield for a corner, I´d propably need a taxi to get back"

Jimmy' Greaves

"He's looking around at himself"

Jimmy Hill

"Despite the rain, it's still raining here at Old Trafford"

João Pinto

"At one point of the match we felt like we were at the edge of a cliff... but we managed to do the right thing and stepped forward"

Joe Cole

"Bon match pour... my team – mon équipe – et... I'm very happy"

Joe Kinnear

"Shola Amamobi (31) is getting better and better, he's a young kid"

"I can count on the fingers of one hand ten games where we've caused our own downfall"

Joe Marston

"I recall once cutting my knee in the snow and at half-time they put some whisky on the wound, gave me a sip, and sent me back out"

Joe Royle

"Balotelli is like Marmite, you love him or hate him. Me, I'm between"

Joey Barton

"Depending who you listen to I'm a footballer, ex-con, ranting anti-celebrity, football's philosopher king, loving Dad and violent thug all rolled into one"

"Have to take back what I said about Thiago Silva being over-rated today. Been immense tonight. Still looks like an overweight ladyboy though!"

"Baffles me, which way he's (Thiago Silva) going. Is he a man changing to a woman or a woman changing to a man? Can't work it out"

"Neymar is the Justin Bieber of football"

Johann Cruyff

"Coincidence is logical"

"You have got to shoot, or you can't score"

"Actually I never make a mistake, because it takes a huge effort for me to be wrong"

"The goalie is the first attacker, and the striker the first defender"

"If you play on possession, you don´t have to defend, because there´s only one ball"

"Technique is not being able to juggle a ball 1000 times. Anyone can do that by practicing. Then you can work in the circus"

"If you want to play quicker you can start running faster, but it´s the ball that decides the speed of the game"

"In small space a player has to be capable of acting quickly. A good player who needs too much time can suddenly become a poor player"

"Football is a game you play with your brain"

"The cleverest do maths, the next best write books. Dancers are the cleverest with their feet, next are footballers"

"It's all very simple: if you score one more than your opponent, you win"

"Italians can never win from you, but you can lose to them"

John Barnes

"If Glen Hoddle had been any other nationality, he would have had 70 or 80 caps for England"

John Hartson

"Playing every week helps any player improve their game"

"I have never been one to just turn up and be a part of the furniture"

John Hollins

"A contract on a piece of paper, saying you want to leave, is like a piece of paper saying you want to leave"

John Toshack

"Winning all the time is not necessarily good for the team"

"It was always going to be hard but it may even be a bit harder now"

"He's played every game for Manchester City this season including two hours at Doncaster"

Johnny Giles

"I'd rather play in front of a full house than an empty crowd"

Jorge Domínguez

"Football is passion, multitude, the joy of living"

Jorge González

"I've never considered myself to be an example to follow. I like to live life in my own way. I'm not one for conforming, or adhering to the logical approach that comes with appropriate behaviour"

Jorge Valdano

"Coaches who talk all day about the fight and the struggle have little to teach"

"In Spain the great forwards, like the best perfumes of the world, come in a small container"

"The bacillus of efficiency has also attacked football, and some dare to ask what´s the point in playing well. I feel tempted to tell about the time they dared to ask Borges what is poetry for, to which he answered: What is a sunrise for? What are caresses for? What is the smell of coffee for? Each question sounded like a sentence. They are for pleasure, for emotion, for living"

"I'm not haunted by either past frustrations or former glories, I think it's very important to know how to turn over a new leaf once your footballing career is over. Letting yourself get bogged down in nostalgia is dangerous"

"What sets me apart is that I've done a bit of everything within football"

"All my dreams came true, but a footballer's career is not just about fulfilling ambitions. It's also about struggle and frustration, which teach you more than when your dreams become reality"

"Romario is like a cartoon soccer player"

"Football is an excuse to make us happy"

"If we have to travel from point A to point B, everyone would take the six-lane highway and get there as quickly as possible. Everyone, except Riquelme. He would would choose the winding mountain road"

José Mourinho

"Please don´t call me arrogant, but I´m European champion and I think I ´m a special one"

"We are in contention for a lot of trophies because of my hard work"

"Everybody was waiting for Chelsea not to win every game and one day when we lose there will be a holiday in the country"

"There is no pressure at the top. The pressure's being second or third"

"I am Jose Mourinho and I don´t change. I arrive with all my qualities and my defects"

"Fear is not a word in my football dictionary"

"I´m a coach. I´m not Harry Potter"

"I studied Italian five hours a day for many months to ensure I could communicate with the players, media and fans. Ranieri had been in England for five years and still struggled to say good morning and good afternoon"

"I´ve reached the conclusion that I am good loser."

"Young players are a little bit like melons. Only when you open and taste the melon are you 100% sure that the melon is good"

"My history as a manager cannot be compared with Frank Rijkaard´s history. He has zero trophies and I have a lot of them"

"The moral of the story is not to listen to those who tell you not to play the violin but stick to the tambourine"

"Even Jesus Christ wasn't liked by everyone. What hope is there for me?"

"It seems like Tottenham came to Stamford Brige by bus and they parked it in front of their goal"

"It´s not even a game between me and him (Cristiano Ronaldo). It´s a game where a kid made some statements not showing maturity and respect. Maybe it´s his difficult childhood, no education, maybe it´s the consequence of that"

Josef Herberger

"The ball is round, the game lasts ninety minutes, and everything else is just theory"

Jozy Altidore

"I demand more of myself. I'm freezing up in front of goal lately"

"English football is all about desire and fighting"

Juan Arango

"The goals of the Venezuelan National Team are always spectacular"

Juan Mata

"The thing I like most about Manchester United is that they brought me here by helicopter"

Juan Román Riquelme

"Ten is just a number, I do not look back when I play"

Juan Sebastián Verón

"Tell the fans to enjoy themselves. I will give nothing but the best"

Juanito

"Ninety minutes in the Bernabeu are very long"

Jun'ichi Inamoto

"I can understand everyone. Everyone except Ray Parlour"

Junior

"This is a game for men. If you're scared, get it right"

Jürgen Klinsmann

"A baker cannot live on bread he made yesterday, and a footballer cannot live on his last game. It's about the here and now"

"Obviously, you want more in the Champions League, where the music is played"

Jürgen Klopp

"I told my players during the break - Since we´re here anyway, we might actually play a bit of football"

"The reason Gotze is leaving? He wants to work with this extraordinary coach that is Guardiola. So if it´s anyone's fault it's mine. I cannot make myself 15cm shorter and speak Spanish"

"In my playing career I never succeeded in bringing to the field what was going on in my brain. I had the talent for the 5th division, and the mind for the Bundesliga. The result was a career in the 2nd division"

"I congratulate every fan who has persevered through our game in Cottbus until the end in front of the television"

"Maybe he (Florentino Perez) just doesn't know in the mornings what he is about to do with his money when the evening comes"

"When we played here 2 years,we had 5 people in front of our hotel when we arrived. This year, there were 20! We improved!"

"He (Arsene Wenger) likes having the ball, playing football, passes... it's like an orchestra. But it is a silent song. I like heavy metal more. I always want it loud"

"If I had a bigger budget, I'd sign Ibrahimovic. I like crazy players and they seem to like me"

Just Fontaine

"The best (Real Madrid) I ever saw, apart from Brazil"

Kaká

"Faith that decides whether something will happen or not"

"It was a time in which I learned you have to give your best every single day because the next day you might not be able"

"If things happen it's because God has prepared me. God has great things for us. If it's God's will that I be there, there I will be"

Kalusha Bwalya

"Sometimes, it's only when you reach deep into your own soul, that something special comes out"

Karel Poborsky

"I do not miss the game – my time is over. What I really miss is moving"

Kasey Keller

"I spent four years at Millwall so I'm sure thats prepared me for whatever happens on Sunday (IRAN-USA WC 1998)"

"If you're not up, if you're not ready to perform, you're not going to win"

Keisuke Honda

"Japanese never give up, they have a strong mentality, they are very disciplined, so do have the right characteristics and this will be something I will take on to the pitch with me"

Keith Hill

"People might start respecting the job I'm doing on limited resources - and I mean really limited"

"You can compare us at the moment to a bit of soft porn – there is an awful lot of foreplay and not a lot going on in the box"

Ken Charlery

"It (Wembley) was strange, it was a very, very big massive changing room and shower area with double baths, showers, everything huge, like four rooms into one - even a little bar in the corner"

"Just take advice from your coaches and experienced players and you shouldn't go far wrong"

Kenneth Asamoah Boateng

"I love listening to gospel music, reading my bible - and watching football"

Kenny Cunningham

"You become a little bit more vocal with age and people will probably tell you when I was younger that I was a bit more shy"

"Arsenal's defence will be a worry going forward"

"That kind of natural understanding doesn't develop naturally"

Kevin Betsy

"Fickle fans are not helping us"

"I lost the ball in the second half and I could hear the ooohs... It was like I had killed someone"

Kevin Keegan

"There'll be no siestas in Madrid tonight"

"It's like a toaster, the ref's shirt pocket. Every time there's a tackle, up pops a yellow card"

"Chile have three options - they could win or they could lose"

"The ref was vertically 15 yards away"

"I don't think there is anybody bigger or smaller than Maradona"

"We deserved to win this game after hammering them 0-0 in the first half"

"There's a slight doubt about only one player, and that's Tony Adams, who definitely wont be playing tomorrow"

"The ref was vertically 15 yards away"

"I don't think there is anybody bigger or smaller than Maradona"

"I don't think they're as good as they are"

"They're the second best team in the world, and there's no higher praise than that"

"I don't think they're as good as they are"

"I was at a social function with him (Romeo Benetti) the other week, and it's the first time I've got within ten yards of him and he hasn't kicked me. Even then I kept looking over my shoulder"

"England has the best fans in the world and Scotland's fans are second-to-none"

"I came to Nantes two years ago and it's much the same today, except that it's completely different"

"I'll never play at Wembley again, unless I play at Wembley again"

"The 33 or 34-year-olds will be 36 or 37 by the time the next World Cup comes around, if they're not careful"

"The only way we will get into Europe is by ferry"

"I know what is around the corner – I just don't know where the corner is"

Khodadad Azizi

"Our people love football and we are never short of talented players"

Koki Mizuno

"Shunsuke (Nakamura) warned me to become a Great Celtic player. I must not touch alcohol and chips. But I tried them one night and I won´t be doing that again"

Kolo Touré

"We just need now to keep calm and do what we have been doing"

Koo Ja-cheol

"I just have to win the battle with myself"

Landon Donovan

"Most of us are here for more than just playing soccer. We're in it for the bigger goal, to move it along for the next generation"

"I love winning and any team I'm on, I expect to win"

Lasha Salukvadze

"(Dimitri) Cheryshev should train children. He trained children in Spain and that was his real job"

Lee Dixon

"He's sort of facing the goal with his chest"

Lee Dong-Gook

"When you play overseas, sometimes you don't play well because you're nervous"

"Why do you do this? Leave me alone. If I'm goingoverseas, I'll tell you before I go, so please don't write your reports by guessing"

Lee Hendrie

"I took a whack on my left ankle, but something told me it was my right"

Leo Beenhakker

"Football is not played on paper, it is played on a pitch. This game is not mathematics and in football, two plus two very rarely equals four – it's usually three or five"

"A miracle to be here (WC 2006)?, No, we just came by plane"

"When I worked with Trinidad & Tobago at the last World Cup I woke up every morning to the sound of Bob Marley, now I wake up every day suffering from a headache!"

Leon Andreasen

"Maybe if there is a bomb in the dressingroom and four players broke their legs, then I might get to play"

Les Ferdinand

"I was surprised, but I always say nothing surprises me in football"

Lesly Fellinga

"My family was very proud of me and on Haiti. They say when you play for Haiti you have to give everything you got"

Lev Yashin

"The joy of seeing Yuri Gagarin flying in space is only superseded by the joy of a good penalty save"

Lewis Holtby

"I had never heard of Sheriff Tiraspol before – I thought they were from Northern Ireland"

Lionel Messi

"When all this is over, what are you left with? When I retire, I hope I am remembered for being a decent guy"

"Talent and elegance mean nothing without rigor and precision"

"The day you think there are no improvements to be made, is a sad one for any player"

"English clubs are physical and tough, and they play strong for the whole game. But afterwards they shake hands and they are fair"

"Something deep in my character allows me to take the hits and get on with trying to win"

Li Xiaopeng

"Hard work is the only ladder from which you can climb to the peak of success and even then a player with the best attributes can't always achieve greatness without sustained efforts"

Lloyd Doyley

"I've only played for Watford, so I'm called a one-man club"

Lothar Matthäus

"I never blame the trainer for failure. The team is always responsible for wins and losses"

Louis van Gaal

"Louis van Gaal has nothing more to learn"

"I´ve signed a contract with the Dutch national team until 2006. So I can win the World Cup not once but twice"

Lucas Radebe

"When you scream from excitement and everyone is screaming with you, you are one"

"They (Kaizer Chiefs) came to ask me if they could name their band after my former club. I remember they looked like quite scruffy students. I said 'sure', but they needed to change the Z to an S because the real Kaizer (Motaung) would not be happy"

Ludovic Giuly

"I deserved more respect. Apparently I am not even part of the 30 or 40-man list (WC 2006). I don't know where I am and I don't know whether I am part of any plans in the future. So I am off to Australia for a month. I will do some canoeing among crocodiles, kangaroos and penguins"

Luis Figo

"In football, day in day out, you always have to show your worth"

"To play for Barcelona, means to have an opportunity for a brilliant career. But to reach the top of it, you have to play for Real Madrid"

Luis Chavarria

"Happy for my debut, I did well and luckily could injure (Enzo) Francescoli"

Luis Suarez

"In Latin America the border between soccer and politics is vague. There is a long list of governments that have fallen or been overthrown after the defeat of the national team"

"The press have made me feel bad since the moment I arrived in England, they have never judged me on how I play football, they judged me on my attitude"

"It's a huge honour to wear No 7 at Liverpool. I think about the legends: Dalglish, Keegan and that Australian guy"

Luis De Agustini

"Gaddafi's a great bloke. The media only show the bad things. I used to go round his house. His son's a super simple guy. All the Gaddafis were very down to earth"

Luiz Felipe Scolari

"For John Terry, to die on the pitch would be glory. You would need to kill him and maybe even then he'd still play"

"I've had enough of players who are like cassava plants - they just stay rooted to the spot in midfield"

"We often need more one group, than one star"

Lukas Podolski

"I speak German, Polish, English and the local Cologne dialect, you can cope with that combination everywhere. Additionally, you don't play football because of the language, but because there is a ball"

"The problem in Germany is that people don't respect you when you are out with your family. They take pictures and even when you say 'No' they take, take, take"

"Football is like chess, only without the dice"

Luke Wilkshire

"That's football. It doesn't always go to plan"

"I didn't expect half the things that have happened in my life. You dream about it, but you don't necessarily believe that they're going to come true"

Luther Blisset

"No matter how much money you have here (Milan), you can't seem to get Rice Krispies"

Ma Minguy

"It was a pity I was not given any playing time with Perugia, but I gained exposure to top-level football by training with the team"

Maksim Shatskikh

"I think, the coach can count on me"

Malcolm MacDonald

"Mirandinha will have more shots this afternoon than both sides put together"

Manucho Gonçalves

"The main think is helping the team achieve the goal"

Manuel Neuer

"After some games this season, I haven't needed to have a shower. Yes, I guess sometimes it is boring being in goal (Bayern Munchen)"

Marc Overmars

"Good players never want to sit on the bench as substitutes"

Marcel Desailly

"In winter, when it's raining and you have to go and play a small team in the north, I won't reveal what passes through your mind when you're getting out of the bus"

Marcelino Elena

"The fans called me a ´Thieving Spaniard´"

Marcello Lippi

"They (Florentine fans) were rude about my mother, the poor woman, who is from Florence. But I do think they could leave my father alone. He died six years ago"

"I have to be optimistic, I have no choice"

"I will not pick players on reputation alone."

Marcelo Balboa

"I was always taught as a kid if you do something, do it right. If not, go do something else. For me, soccer was life"

Marcelo Bielsa

"Football is less exciting when played by those who know how to play"

"Everything that football generates, it generates because of that desire to capture the emotion of those who cry when their team wins or loses"

Marian Pahars

"I'm glad I'm still playing because at some stage I thought it might be over"

Mario Balotelli

"I'm not a bad guy but I'm shy"

"Mourinho is the best coach in the world, but as a man he still needs to learn manners and respect"

"They didn't get angry because I was booked for taking my shirt off, but they saw my physique and got jealous"

"You want to compare me to Ibra? Well, that's a compliment – for him!"

"Mario got it wrong and Mario apologises, but I don't want to apologise to everyone because it's not as if I killed someone"

"I'm genius – I'm Different. If you can find another like me, I'll buy you dinner!"

"When I score, I don't celebrate because I'm only doing my job. When a postman delivers letters, does he celebrate?"

Mario Götze

"People call me the German Messi, I prefer being called the German Cristiano Ronaldo"

Mario Jardel

"A classico is a classico and vice versa"

Mario Kempes

"One player on his own is not going to win you the World Cup"

Mario Mandžukić

"I want to go to my limits"

Mário Zagallo

"They say Ronaldo is fat. Well, I for one would love to have eleven 'fat' players like Ronaldo in my side"

"We'll be the first to arrive and the last to leave"

"I'm optimistic - but not much"

"I'm addicted to winning"

Mark Bright

"There was nothing wrong with his timing - he was just a bit late"

Mark Draper

"I'd like to play for an Italian club, like Barcelona"

Mark Lawreson

"He can be as good as he wants to be, that's how good he can be"

"(Kevin) Kilbane's like a one-eyed cat in a fish shop - he doesn't know what to do or where to go"

"Liverpool have finished fourth, third and second, so if they finish fifth it'll be an average season for them"

"Fernando Torres needs to be loved on a regular basis"

"Looks like he's (Per Mertesacker) pulling an old fridge when he runs"

Mark McGhee

"We stayed in a hotel (Albania) and I remember Dougie Bell vacating his room because it was full of of cockroaches. We ate mars bars and cornflakes for the duration of our stay"

Mark Viduka

"I would not be bothered if we lost every game as long as we won the league"

"I am a Libra so I have to balance things"

Marc Wilmots

"I have no regrets and I'd do everything the same way again - I've always been able to make my own decisions, and they've always chimed with my mentality and my sporting ability"

"To do this job, you have to be passionate and love the game and tactics"

"I'm nobody. I'm nothing at all. Like everyone else, I will die one day and finish up in a wooden box"

Marco Borriello

"I must admit I have a dressingroom curiosity over Beckham. I want to see if he is equipped as he is in the underwear advertisements"

Mart Poom

"I've played more international games for Estonia than I have for Arsenal"

Martin Dahlin

"My motivation and my back no longer exist"

"I´ve played my last match, scored my last goal and elbowed my last opponent"

Martin Jol

"Anything can happen at Highbury. Maybe hundreds of squirrels will come on to the pitch and we will have a problem. You cannot prepare for things like that"

Martin O'Neill

"I think I am the bad cop and I think he (Roy Keane) is the bad, bad cop"

Martin Skertl

"I have to say that the Everton fans respect us, of course it´s different on derby matches"

Martin Vunk

"What can we do if Estonian refs are so shitty"

Masami Ihara

"I always say you never know what will happen in football"

Massimo Maccarone

"The football ground is my arena, my colosseum, and it doesn't matter if I am fighting lions or men, I feel like I am the gladiator"

Matt Busby

"It was a very simple team talk. All I used to say was: Whenever possible, give the ball to George Best"

Mazinho

"Being the moral victor means nothing – what matters is the title"

Mesut Özil

"Wenger had bids turned down for a new coat"

"I don't need criticism to improve my performances. I don't play football to try and prove someone wrong. I have nothing to prove. I play football because I like doing so"

Michael Ballack

"It may be an advantage for us that we are hard assess"

Michael Dawson

"We need to start working better individually as a team"

Mihael Essien

"I call him daddy (Jose Mourinho) because I see him as like a father"

Michael Laudrup

"If you win then it cures everything, it's a mechanism of the football world"

Michael Owen

"I don´t believe in superstitions. I just do certain things because I´m scared in case something will happen if I don´t do them"

"I was really surprised when the FA knocked on my doorbell"

Michalis Konstantinou

"I am delighted with what I achieved in my career. It's been great and even the criticism was welcome because that helped me along the way. We will see what the future holds"

Michel Hildago

"Even his (Platini) feet are intelligent"

Michel Platini

"What Zidane can do with a football, Maradona could do with an orange"

"Football is made up of mistakes, because a perfect match is 0-0"

"When Germany plays bad, they go to final. When they play well they win it"

"The street is the best way to become a good footballer"

"Doping is like making love, you need two to do it – the doctor and the athlete"

Mick McCarthy

"I was feeling as sick as the proverbial donkey"

"I've slept with a coat hanger in my mouth to keep the smile on my face"

"In the first half, I didn't see the second half coming - that's for sure"

Micky Quinn

"Luis Suarez is a victim of his own make-up"

"Possession stats at one point were 77 per cent to 33 per cent"

Miguel Ángel Lotina

"Crowds are fickle, one day they throw you flowers, another day they throw you the flower pot"

Mike Gray

"Well Kerry, you´re 19 and you´re a lot older than a lot of people younger than yourself"

Mike Ingham

"And here goes Aguero, looking to relieve himself"

Mike Summerbee

"Next thing we'll be giving our handbags to the linesmen as we skip onto the field"

Miralem Pjanić

"Mentally I'm fine. I have confidence in my abilities"

"My parents couldn't really afford to buy me toys when I was a kid. My father played semi-professional football, so I always carried around a football.

Mitchell Thomas

"All that remains is for a few dots and commas to be crossed"

Mohamed Al Deayea

"It's not the end of the world (after 8-0 losing to German)"

Mohamed Chaib

"We have serious doubts over the effects of medication that we were given during training camps. We just want the truth"

Mohamed Diame

"It (Wigan) is a crappy place. The town is tiny, and there is no atmosphere. I go in to training, I return home afterwards, and that is all I do"

"It is a myth to claim that all English women are ugly. But I won't lie, it is rare to see truly beautiful girls when you go out during the day"

Mohamed Salah

"I am a footballer – I do not do politics. I respect everybody, it doesn't matter where they come from"

Moritz Volz

"Coverage of football is made up of the same old clichés. But at the end of the day, that's just football, to be fair"

Morten Olsen

"Perhaps it's a bit rough to compare (Denmark's 4-0 defeat to Armenia), but in terms of football, it was our September 11"

Mustafa El Hadji

"The Premier League is like a different planet. Every player should experience it at least once in their career. Football is a religion there."

"I've still got the mindset of a player and it's not easy to be in charge of a group of people"

Muzzy Izzet

"I don't know the words of the national anthem but I enjoy the Turkish culture and the food"

Mykhaylo Fomenko

"We should be fully motivated for every opponents, as we were during World Cup qualification"

Mwepu Ilunga

"I did not have a reason to continue (WC 2010) injured while those who will benefit financially were sitting on the terraces watching"

Mwinyi Kazimoto

"Players from Europe, South America, especially Brazil and Argentina coming here (Quatar). So everyone is committed and I have been fighting to make sure that I give my best to the team"

Nemanja Vidic

"No matter how much silverware you win in your career you always want more"

"In England, they say that Manchester is the city of rain. It's main attraction is considered to the timetable at the railway station, where trains leave for other... less rainy cities"

Neném Prancha

"Brazilian player will have no problem in Mexico. All lived in favela and can not complain about the altitude"

Neville Southall

"If you don't believe you can win, there is no point in getting out of bed at the end of the day"

Neymar

"I have never been concerned about winning the Ballon d'Or"

"It's true that I like to go out and buy new clothes, nice perfumes and hair products. I also shave my legs. I don't see myself as a metrosexual"

"I don´t sell myself for money"

"Cristiano Ronaldo has style, but I'm the handsome one"

Nigel Worthington

"He tried to get a head on it but it came off the wrong corner of his head"

Nikolai Starostin

"Gulag camp bosses, arbiters of the life and death of thousands upon thousands of human beings – were so benevolent to anything concerning football. Their unbridled power over human lives was nothing compared to the power of football over them"

Nicolas Anelka

"If, since the start, I'd played well and put in some good matches. It would all have been too simple"

"Islam helped me to be calm and concentrated and have high morale"

Nicolás Burdisso

"Taking me from behind is something that is not worthy behaviour of a man"

Nikolče Noveski

"I am talking when I feel that I should say something"

Nwankwo Kanu

"We could not always get three meals in a day; sometimes we'd struggle. But we always had soccer. It's something that pulls the whole country together. Something that can bring peace and unity to Nigeria"

Obafemi Martins

"Things have taken time to get used to (Newcastle). The weather's not great and people seem to drink beer all the time, but there´s nowhere I´d rather be playing"

"I did not know of Hull. I know nothing. Maybe with my satellitenavigator I could find it. I would have no idea where it is on the map."

Obdulio Varela

"It was a fluke terms: stolen title from Brazilian (WC 1950). Such things happen only once"

"I did not like to see those 200,000 fans sad"

Ole Gunnar Solskjær

"I am not a dribbling winger like Ryan Giggs or George Best was so I don't think you will see me with too much chalk on my boots"

"Kjetil (Rekdal), who was my room-mate, told me: 'Ole, tonight I'm going to score in the last minute with a penalty.' And that's exactly what happened! So, maybe there is something about inklings and destinies, but I suppose we'll never know"

Oleg Blokhin

"You (journalist) should respect that I played football? Did you play football? Respect my job and me. I won't allow anyone to criticise my team. If you're a man, go with me. One on one"

Oliver Kahn

"When you look at our programme for the next few weeks, you do not fancy a trip to Oktoberfest"

"If we perform as a unit and if every single player gives his best, everything can happen"

"Big matches on the big stage are often decided at the back"

"If we perform as a unit and if every single player give it his very best, everything can happen"

Olivier Karekezi

"There is no such thing as Hutu or Tutsi now - we are all together"

Ondino Viera

"Other countries have their history. Uruguay has its football"

Osvaldo Ardiles

"The fact that Arsene Wenger took everybody to the Champions League final apart from Walcott says a lot. He even took the tea-lady"

"Glenn (Hoddle) is putting his head in the frying pan"

Otto Rehhagel

"The differences between the big teams and the so-called smaller teams have become smaller"

"There are no right or wrong, or fair results. There's just the final score"

"Sometimes, you lose and sometimes the other team wins"

Paolo Di Canio

"Let's be honest. We're (Sheffield Wednesday) not Manchester United or Arsenal, are we?"

"If they have more desire and if they play less empty in the brain, they can keep the ball much better. At this moment they are empty"

"I was too good, my level was too high - It would be stupid for a chairman not to call me"

"I am a fascist, not a racist. I give the straight arm salute because it is a salute from a 'camerata' to 'camerati'. The salute is aimed at my people. With the straight arm I don't want to incite violence and certainly not racial hatred"

"I said if you (referee) want to complete a perfect job, you can send me off. He took it seriously and sent me off"

"The man who comes to take care of my piranhas tells me he will kill all my fish if I leave West Ham"

Paolo Maldini

"You need to learn to separate your professional life from your private life"

"We burn referees like that at the stake"

Paolo Rossi

“God bless whoever invented football. It was the English, I think. And what a fantastic idea it was”

"The Dutch change positions quicker than you can make a cup of coffee"

Pauleta

”It’s true that I’d always aimed to play for a big club in Portugal but later, after I turned 30, it began to make less and less sense”

Paulo Roberto Falcão

”People want to go to the stadium to watch a good show and win just is not enough just to have fun”

Park Chu-Young

“I just want to show how good I am and prove myself."

”I remember my second day in Vigo. I decided to go and have a look around the city and, when I was standing at Plaza Compostela, in front of the Nagari Hotel, someone passed by me and then came back to ask me if I needed anything. That really surprised me because I thought that it was really kind”

Pascoal Silva Cinelli

"I can not leave my family (and go to WC) in Brazil suffering the torments of hunger"

Pasi Rautiainen

"If a man's name is Trabelsi, I guess it mean just troubles"

"Well, you know how it feels when such a big black men (Toure and Eboue) comes to the front and behind, it's not nice"

"Champions League was seen several times Rüştü (Reçber) excerpts from the early 2000's, but before the UEFA Euro (2008) I was sure that this gentleman is already selling rugs in the bazaars of Istanbul"

"Liverpool had to put long balls to Crouch who put them from the depth to the small mickymouses"

"Torres smelled the roast in the oven"

Pat Crerand

"Matt (Busby) was the eternal optimist. In 1968 he still hoped that Glen Miller was just mssing"

Patric Oboya

"Fans are the reason why we go to the pitch every day, training hard"

Patrick Vieira

"Everyone thinks he (Ruud Van Nistelrooy) is a nice guy, but he is a son of a bitch"

Patrice Evra

"People have a good impression of me, it won't be these tramps (Bixente Lizarazu) who dirty my image"

"And what's the other one called, Screwdriver? Rolland (Courbis) Screwdriver. All he does is talk"

"That was the first time I used my right foot. I normally only use it just to walk on the bus!"

"I always tell Cristiano (Ronaldo) before training, 'If you do stepovers on me, I will break your legs and rip up your shirt.' I have no wish to have the mickey taken out of me all week"

"He sullied my name without trying to find out what happened. Lilian (Thuram) thinks he's the new coach, the president of the federation and the president of the (French) Republic… Walking around with books on slavery in glasses and a hat does not turn you into Malcolm X"

Paul Pogba

"It was the feeling I had with the coach. He said he trusted me, but he didn't let me play. He said I was too young. He said: 'Your time will come' It didn't come"

Paul Elliott

"Bayern will have the added advantage of playing in their own stadium - that's like a home game for them"

"Cahill went off, then Botswana came on"

Paul Gascoine

"I never make predictions, and I never will"

"I've had 14 bookings this season - 8 of which were my fault, but 7 of which were disputable"

Paul Ince

"We have to be careful not to let our game not be the game we know it should be"

"I am happy to be a role model for anybody - whether they are black, white, yellow, pink or purple"

"Ferguson is a gent from Monday to Friday. Saturday out comes the beast"

"I love tackling, love it. It's better than sex"

Paul Merson

"Reading won't have the confidence to be confident"

"When Everton knock it long, they don't knock it long"

"As the saying goes: 'you don't fix something if it isn't broken'"

"There's only one person gets you sacked and that's the fans"

"Football's all about yesterday, it's all about now"

Paul Put

"You have to be big when you lose and humble when you win"

"There were a lot of doubters when I first arrived in Ouagadougou to take up my post. I believe many were hoping for a Jose Mourinho-type coach, not Paul Put"

Paul Robinson

"If I could be a superhero, I would be Batman. He's got the least silly tights"

Paulin Voavy

"This is the first time in my career that I take a red card and especially in this way"

Paulo Wanchope

"If the coach and the team are attacked from all sides, then you just wait for the right moment to strike back with full force"

Pavel Nedved

"It's not just about skill and hard work, you need a football brain to be effective"

Pelé

"Success is no accident. It is hard work, perseverance, learning, studying, sacrifice and most of all, love of what you are doing or learning to do"

"One of the greatest things I see in Sócrates is his ability to play better football backwards than when facing the front. In that area he´s unique"

"Yes, Ronaldinho is bigger than me. Exactly 4 centimeter"

"I don´t believe there is such a thing as a 'born' soccer player. Perhaps you are born with certain skills and talents, but quite frankly it seems impossible to me that one is actually born to be an ace soccer player"

"I score more than thousend goals in my life, but the goal I don´t score they remember"

Pepe Reina

"Carra (Jamie Carragher) doesn't like me to fist him before the games, so I give him a high-five instead"

Perry Groves

"Gareth Bale has been levitated to the status of one of the best players in the world"

Peter Crouch

"Had I not become a footballer – I would have been a virgin"

Peter Odemwingie

"Coloured players feel the open racism there (Russia)"

Peter Osgood

"Di Matteo's taken to playing in midfield like a duck out of water"

Peter Schmeichel

"In football you sometimes have beauty and cruelty together"

"If I spend the whole of this week thinking about Brazil and all their great players, I would probably be terrified by Friday"

"You have to believe you can win"

"Wake up every morning, be happy that you are here and achieve as much as you can every day"

Peter Shilton

"If you stand still there is only one way to go, and that's backwards"

"You've got to believe that you're going to win and I believe we'll win the World Cup until the final whistle blows and we're knocked out"

"The main factor in a penalty shoot-out is luck. You need to stay calm and focused but the biggest thing you need is luck"

"Being fit will keep you mentally sharp and people forget that"

"As a goalkeeper you need to be good at organising the people in front of you and motivating them. You need to see what's going on and react to the threats. Just like a good manager in business"

Peter Taylor

"When I said even my Missus could save Derby from relegation, I was exaggerating"

"What I saw in Holland and Germany was that the majority of people are Dutch in Holland and German in Germany"

"Football is all about winning, drawing and losing"

Peter Withe

"Both sides have scored a couple of goals, and both sides have conceded a couple of goals"

Petter Rudi

"One point from an away game is no longer considered a victory"

Phil Brown

"If you closed your eyes, you couldn't tell the difference between the two sides"

Phil Neal

"It's a case of putting all our eggs into the next ninety minutes"

"Whoever you support, you've got that blood in your veins"

Phil Neville

"The Brazilians were South America, and the Ukranians will be more European"

"There is only one Alex Ferguson, but there are similarities"

Phil Thompson

"Ronnie Moran had us as young boys, religiously"

"(Adam) Bogdan should be playing for whatever country he comes from"

Phil Woosnam

"The rules of soccer are very simple, basically it is this: if it moves, kick it. If it doesn´t move, kick it until it does"

Philipp Lahm

"You have to learn to live with the public criticism"

"Sport is not just recreational fun. Sport is like a language that is understood around the world"

Phenyo Mongala

"We have disappointed but we have learnt our lesson"

Pierre Van Hoijdonk

"It may be good enough (transfer payment) for the homeless, but not for an international striker"

Pierre Wome

"They wanted to and could have killed me (after missing penalty). I have never been afraid of death, my concern was about the safety of my relatives"

Pierangelo Manzaroli

"We'll try to be at the top of our game, but we know it's hard for us (San Marino) to get points"

Pierre-Emerick Aubameyang

"It's nice (score goals), but at the end of the day it's not important who scores"

Pinga

"The Hungarian defense is the same as a open door"

Radamel Falcao

"I've prepared myself mentally and physically in the training sessions to be a complete player"

"Our world is not real, football is strange. People don't see the bad times"

"I am calm - I don't even know what I'm doing tomorrow"

Rafael Benítez

"I talk to Carra, if you can understand him you can understand anyone"

"I've learned that you have to score goals to win games"

Rafael Márquez

"Before Pep (Guardiola) arrived, the changing room was not good, so he had to bring a little bit of order back and he did that pretty well"

"I'm enjoying myself, there's (New York Red Bulls) not so much pressure and I can not pay more attention to my family"

Rafael Van der Vaart

"What the hell am I doing here (HSV)?"

Rafinha

"I like to pull it out when I score, it's how I celebrated when I scored goals in derby matches in Brazil and Germany as well"

Ramon Quiroga

"I am Argentine by birth, but Peruvian in heart. Peru can trust my honesty"

Rauf Inileev

"I think the most important thing which the national team got during my tenure was the respect and recognition of the fans"

"The most amazing thing is: As a player I was a defender but my teams and clubs always want to show attacking football. I am focused on attacking game"

"In recent years football has become an industry and we all depend on results"

Raúl

"I think I'm OK. I'm very optimistic and in good shape physically. I only need a goal to make me feel calmer"

"When I go five games without a goal, there's always a debate. Everything else that I do on the pitch is never valued"

"Thank you from all my football heart and Hala Madrid!"

Ray Houghton

"Ji-Sung Park is probably not as young as he was when he arrived at Old Trafford all those years ago"

Ray Hudson

"I've got nothing to say. Any questions?"

Ray Parlour

"The last six games of the Invincibles season were the most pressurised, because we were under pressure"

"Martin Jol has put his hands on his heads"

"Southampton have always been at the top, apart from the seasons when they weren't"

Ray Stubbs

"If you were in the Brondby dressing room right now, which of the Liverpool players would you be looking at?"

Raymond Domenech

"I do not know what he (Materazzi) said to Zidane. Know only that he was the man of the match, not Pirlo. He tied the game and sent Zidane off"

Rene Adler

"To our fans, I'm sorry you had to pay money for this shit"

Ricardinho

"I make a goal as Luiz Felipe (Scolari) want"

Ricardo Gardner

"I've been keeping myself healthy to prepare for what God has in store for me in the future"

Ricardo La Volpe

"I wonder if most of them even realise a game is going on. My grandmother could play better than them"

"The first team to make a mistake would not win"

Ricardo Lopez

"There's a rumour in Spain that United players have to wear special red underwear with a Vodafone logo on it. I can tell you that I haven´t seen anything like that yet but if I have to wear it I will"

Richard Møller Nielsen

"English football has a class, a decency to it which does not exist anywhere else in the world"

"Love is good for footballers, as long as it is not at half-time"

Richard Rufus

"It was like the ref had a brand new yellow card and wanted to see if it worked"

Richard Witschge

"While sitting on the bench you develop strange thoughts. You hope certain team mates play rubbish. Or get an injury. Not a painful one, but one that lasts very long. You feel like a gas station owner hoping that his competitor's station burns down"

Rinus Michels

"Football is war"

Rio Ferdinand

"Our lives are quite boring. I spend a lot of time watching Coronation Street and Eastenders"

"Danny Mills is the oldest 24-year old I´ve ever met. He wears pyjamas, slippers - everything your grandad would wear"

Rivaldo

"My time belongs to God now. My life in Angola is about more than soccer. God is here"

Robbie Fowler

"It's looking more and more less likely"

Robbie Keane

"I can't even remember when the Seventies was"

Robert Pirès

"For a professional sportsman, being injured is like living in a stranger's body"

Roberto Baggio

"It's better to have ten disorganized players than ten organized runners"

"I have lost three World Cups, all on penalties. If you'll allow me this - it really gets on my nerves"

Roberto Carlos

"I'm so glad there will now be two good-looking guys (Beckham signed) at Real. I've felt so lonely in such an ugly team"

Roberto Di Matteo

"In the FA Cup, you always have to expect the unexpectable"

Roberto Dinamite

"This thing of moral champion does not exist (WC 1978)"

Roberto Martinez

"The draws were more victories without goals"

Roberto Perfumo

"For a football player there is nothing better than another football player ... whenever they are in the same team"

Robin Van Persie

"Our fellow players are sometimes occupying the spaces I want to play in. And when I see that, it makes it difficult for me to come to those spaces as well. So that forces me to adjust my runs, based on the position of my fellow players. And, unfortunately - they are often playing in my zones. I think that's a shame"

Robinho

"At the time, I thought I was joining Manchester United from Real Madrid. I wasn't aware there was another Manchester club"

"They treat me like Maradona over here. I hope I can repay all this love on the field. I just can´t score any goals by hand"

"I haven't got a Maradona doll that I stick pins in every day, I don't need psychiatric help"

"For me the best team is one where you get to play"

Rodney Marsh

"It's not fair to say Lee Bowyer's a racist. He'd stamp on anyone's head"

Roger Milla

"I only really watch sport. That´s where you see real joy I don´t like watching mutch else on TV, because it´s generally either twisted or sad"

"When you start out as a professional footballer it's a bit like a journey into the unknown"

"It's thanks to football that a small country could become great"

"I admire our President. He is our President. When he goes there will be another President whom I will admire"

Rolf Rüssmann

"Alright, if we can't beat them, we could at least ruin their pitch"

Romário

"God created me to delight people with goals"

"The coach should keep out of the way - He is an important figure, of course, but is more likely to lose a match than win it. Matches are won by players"

"When I was born, God pointed at me and said That´s The Man"

"Pele with his mouth shut is the worlds greatest poet"

"Will I become a coach in the future? No way. I´d never be able to put up with someone like me"

"What´s the point of running a few minutes at 9 AM in the morning? They say everybody else has to do it. But I'm not everybody else"

"I'm like money, at the end of the day everybody quite likes me"

"Why should I practice if when I get on the pitch I know exactly what to do?

"I'm with 72 kg, yes, so what? Elephant is fat, but when you have forest fire, nobody wins him in the race"

Romelu Lukaku

"I always wore the same shoes as Didier (Drogba) and I subscribed to Chelsea TV to watch these clips they show of training. We have the same hair"

"Eden Hazard's English is catastrophic. I asked him: 'Are you happy with your transfer?' He said: 'I don't understand!'"

Romerito

"I'm not a great soloist. But I have a pretty complete game"

Ronaldinho

"I have the chance to do for a living what I like the most in life, and that's playing football. I can make people happy and enjoy myself at the same time"

"God gives gifts to everyone. Some can write, some can dance. He gave me the skill to play football and I am making the most of it"

"Living in the same era as Messi, that must be the biggest frustration of Cristiano Ronaldo"

Ronaldo

"We lost because we didn´t win"

"I'm sure sex wouldn't be so rewarding as this World Cup. It's not that sex isn't good but the World Cup is every four years and sex is not "

"It is like yesterday when I was still watching the stars of Brazilian football on TV, and I am one of them now"

"When you swap shirts at the end of the match you expect it to smell bad, but Beck's smelt really nice"

"I don't want fans to have the same disappointment as me when I was refused by some players to sign my notebook when I was young"

"There will always be a market for a striker who is fast, scores goals regularly and is strong. I've scored more than 100 goals and people know what they are buying"

Ron Atkinson

"I'm going to make a prediction - it could go either way"

"I never comment on referees and I'm not going to break the habit of a lifetime for that prat"

"I would not say he (David Ginola) is the best left winger in the Premiership, but there are none better"

"He dribbles a lot and the opposition don't like it - you can see it all over their faces"

"They've picked their heads up off the ground and they now have a lot to carry on their shoulders"

"Zero - zero is a big score!"

"You don't want to be giving away free kicks in the penalty area"

Ron Greenwood

"Glenn Hoddle hasn't been the Hoddle we know. Neither has Bryan Robson"

Ronald Maul

"We were already standing in front of the toilet, but still wet our pants"

Ronnie Rosenthal

"I've never been a drinker because it's a different culture from what I was used to, but I tried to fit in and the team spirit at Liverpool"

Ronnie Whelan

"They can see that Croatia are no great shapes"

"He's put on weight and I've lost it, and vice versa"

Roy Hodgson

"We will hope for our best but it is like Forrest Gump and his box of chocolates. We will open it up and see what we get"

"We had a setback against Stoke which set us back a bit"

Roy Keane

"I don´t believe skill was, or ever will be, the result of coaches. It is a result of a love affair between the child and the ball"

"Fail to prepare, prepare to fail"

"I'm not at Manchester United to keep everyone happy"

Roque Máspoli

"The silence after our goal (WC 1950) was something terrible The stadium was dead, and I thought. Brazil will not win"

Rudy Gestede

"I am really enjoying my football and my wife is also happy"

Rüştü Reçber

"Here are three things in life where you do not need a common language - football, music and sex"

Ruud Gullit

"We must have had 99 per cent of the match. It was the other three per cent that cost us"

"A goalkeeper is only a goalkeeper because he can't play football"

Ruud van Nistelrooy

"It's not just the manager who makes the decision, it's the player who makes the decision. They both decide fifty-fifty to make a decision"

Ryan Giggs

"Nelson Mandela is my hero outside of football. I was fortunate enough to meet him a couple of times. He was really clued up on his football and he knew me, so that was just unbelievable. It really stuck with me"

"Football is easy when things are going well"

Saido Berahino

"What we used as a ball was plastic bags wrapped around with laces"

"We left (Burundi). It must have been to do with the civil war and my mum wanting a better life for her kids"

"I'm doing it (football) for my father. I know he's watching me in heaven"

Salvatore Schillaci

"Being striker has become a difficult job. But it is always better than work"

Sam Allardyce

"There are scientists who will tell you that spirit, because it can't be measured, doesn't exist. Bollocks. It does exist"

"Our major problem is that we don't know how to play football"

Sami Al Jaber

"When I scored my first goal ever in the World Cup finals against Morocco in 1994, I never thought or imagined that I was going to score again 12 years later"

Samir Nasri

"I did not show a professional attitude at EURO 2012. But I didn't kill anybody"

"After the EURO, the media attention was very difficult to digest. I'd say that it ruined my season a bit. Everyone talked to me about it. I handled the situation badly, I accept that. I should have given a mea culpa. I shut myself off and, with hindsight, I realise that I was wrong"

Samuel Eto´o

"I'm Samuel Eto'o. I really don't care"

"I'd rather sell groundnuts in my village than to play for a pathetic team like Chelsea"

"He (Beckham) is more beautiful than me, but I 'm a better player"

Samuel Inkoom

"As a team, we fight to win, lose and draw together"

Sándor Kocsis

"Our team lost the Cup because they despised the tournament"

Saphir Taïder

"I made many sacrifices to play abroad at a young age"

Sergio Goycochea

"In my life I've learned to value the importance of hard work"

"There's no manual for footballers that tells them what's going to happen when they retire"

Sergio Ramos

"Football gives you lessons, good and bad. The bad teach more"

Sergio Torres

"At Basingstoke, I would get kicked at least twice every game and people would say things like, 'Go back to Argentina' and insult my Mum"

Sergey Tashuev

"(Will) Danilo disappeared two days before the match played against Illichivets. I didn't have time to work on this issue and to find out what the problem is. This is agents' business, I know nothing. I have no comments right now"

Seo Jung Won

"When it comes to dreaming, I think the bigger the better"

Seydou Doumbia

"Yes, they(CSKA Moscow fans) are noisy and try to put maximum pressure on the opponent, but they make no racist chants. So my fellow (Yaya Touré) Cote d'Ivoire international has obviously overreacted a little bit (official website CSKA)"

Seydou Keita

"I'm afraid for my country, what's happening is not normal. We are all Malians, it's not normal that we kill each others"

"I get goosebumps when speaking of Mali. There is nothing that compares with the joy of giving to a country that is suffering"

Shaka Hislop

"It was like deja vu all over again"

"Mentally, you have to be tough. Keep in mind you are largely remembered for your mistakes. There aren't many players on the pitch who can cope with that fact day in day out, game after game"

"In the Caribbean we touch fists. We were doing that long before Barack Obama"

Shalrie Joseph

"You need to respect winners. For us, all the other sports in Boston have won championships. The Patriots, the Celtics, the Sox, and now hockey too, the Bruins were amazing last year. In a sports town like Boston, if you want to be mentioned with those teams, you need to win championships"

Shane Long

"We have this mentality of going into every game just thinking about the next game"

Shaun Goater

"It's only a matter of time before Manchester City surpass rivals Manchester United as the top team in England"

"When I went back to Bermuda I thought I could leave football behind, but it's a case of a real hunger and I'm missing watching games, and I just really want to be here now"

Shinji Kagawa

"Please ask David Moyes why I'm not in the side"

"I can't tell a word he (Alex Ferguson) says! I am trying to learn English, but understanding the manager might take a little longer"

Shinji Okazaki

"My family and I hold up Japanese traditions, even in Germany"

Shunsuke Nakamur

"Don't just do your best and stop; keep doing your best, keep pushing yourself. That's what makes it possible to realise a dream"

Sifiso Myeni

"When you go to sundown and your career goes down. I don't want to be one of the victims"

Simon Davies

"We knew at half-time we were only half-way there"

Sócrates

"It was like seducing the most beautiful woman in the world. And then failing on the moment for which you did it all"

"In Brazil, the way we live is not like Europe where you have your schedule for the whole year - we don't know what we are doing for the next 15 minutes"

"When I named one of my sons Fidel, my mother said 'that's a bit of a strong name to give a child'. 'Mother,' I said: 'look at what you did to me'"

"I drink, I smoke and I think"

"If Vincent van Gogh and Edgar Degas had known when they were doing their work the level of recognition that they were going to have, they would not have done them the same. You have to enjoy doing the art and not think - will I win?"

"Beauty comes first. Victory is secondary. What matters is joy"

"No player abandons his football career. It´s the football that abandons the player"

"If people do not have the power to say things, then I will say it for them. While I was a footballer, my legs amplified my voice"

Sol Campbell

"You've got to respect every team you play, because many countries can play out of their skins if your underestimate them"

"Everyone feels pressure. It's a question of who can handle it"

Souleymane Diawara

"You should see him (Lucho González) in the changing room: he sings French rap. He's even learn´t the song the Bordeaux fans chant to wind me up: 'Oh, Diawara, go fuck yourself/You have got no loyalty!'"

Sony Norde

"When Sheikh Jamal play in Kolkata, everybody say that they play like Barcelona"

Stan Collymore

"The Bolton back four didn't have a cat on earth's chance"

"Sheikh Mansour is putting his money and his mouth where his mouth is"

"Quite simply, we've got to be honest, there's a very large Polish community in Poland"

Stanley Matthews

"The best (Maradona) one-footed player since Puskas"

"You don't stop playing football because you get old, you get old because you stop playing football"

Stéphane Chapuisat

"Nothing is better than celebrating a trophy with your team mates"

Stéphane Henchoz

"We all speak English, but Carragher talks very strange English

"I'm sure people outside of Switzerland don't understand how we get a team together at all and it certainly doesn't help our chances"

Stevan Jovetić

"The people in my country expect us to beat any team, no matter who they are. I don't know why – but they always expect it!"

Steve Bould

"It sounds ridiculous, but I always put my watch into the right pocket of my trousers. If anybody wants to nick it, they'll know where to look now I suppose"

"I was a scorer of great goals. Great own goals"

Steve Bruce

"I could have another moan but I'm sick to death of my own whining"

Steve Claridge

"They can push the bat a little bit more than others at that level"

Steve Coppell

"If you want to sleep, you don't become a football manager"

Steve Hodge

"Michael Owen is not a diver. He knows when to dive, and when not to"

Steve Lomas

"Germany are a very difficult team to play - they had 11 internationals out there today"

Steve McClaren

"I don't read the papers, I don't gamble, I don't even know what day it is!"

Steven Gerrard

"I'm a fan myself and I'm frustrated just as much as them when we get beat"

"If you don't want success it's not worth playing – winning trophies is the main thing"

"We need to forget about mistakes and take the positives"

"I have a good record there. Played one, won one, and hopefully it will be the same after Saturday"

Steve Sumner

"We didn't know how hot the bath was until we dipped our toes into it"

Stig Inge Bjørnebye

"The left foot has helped - it's always been there, but I haven't always had the chance to use it"

Stuart Murdoch

"I am in a good position at the moment because no-one is running the club. I am hoping there is nobody out there to sack me"

Stuart Pearce

"I can see the carrot at the end of the tunnel"

Subrata Pal

"I don't want to say anything to anyone, but these people should come and see with their own eyes the level of football in the German fourth division and then make their judgement"

Sunday Oliseh

"I'm lucky enough to have had several great years. I can't complain and I thank the good Lord"

Sunil Chhetri

"I never knew that I could make a profession out of football"

Sven-Göran Eriksson

"The midfield is the most crucial area of the game, the one where matches are won or lost"

"Sometimes you have one or two players who are not doing their job, but on this occasion we had about a dozen"

"Football is much harder if you don't have the ball"

Tab Ramos

"(After losing) If we lived in another country we´d need political asylum"

Tam Nsaliwa

”The truth does set you free”

”Football has changed a lot. With all the crisis, the clubs do not giving the opportunity for a player who does not play as regularly as before”

Tarcizio Burgnich

"I thought he (Pele) is made of flesh and bone, like me. I was wrong"

Telê Santana

"Brazilians are not a coward, but the most important thing is to play football”

Terry Butcher

”The beauty of Cup football is that Jack always has a chance of beating Goliath”

Terry Venables

"Certain people are for me and certain people are pro me"

"If history repeats itself, I should think we can expect the same thing again"

”They didn't change positions, they just moved the players around

“There is nothing to be downhearted about, apart from the result”

Theo Walcott

"I've been consistent in patches this season"

"If you're not frustrated that you're not playing football then you shouldn't be playing football"

”If you’re good enough, you’re old enough to play”

Thiago Alcântara

"I would have left Barcelona for any team, just so I would no longer be warming the bench"

Thierry Henry

"Sometimes in football you have to score goals"

"I can't stay in the box and wait for the ball. I can't... I would die"

"Brazilian footballers practice since they birth. They play soccer all day. In French do we studied eight hours a day and when we asked for our mommies if they let us play ball. The answer is always: 'No'"

"It's difficult to talk about Pele because I didn't see him"

"It is true that I can be a pig. It is not a lie to say that. Sometimes, I feel I am in the right even when I'm in the wrong"

"In training you have the press – and they want to come back home and sleep with you"

"I eat football, I sleep football, I breathe football. I'm not mad, I'm just passionate"

Thomas Brolin

"George Graham said just two words to me in six months at Leeds - you´re fired"

Thomas Dooley

"I cut out booze and cigarettes and began to train more, and more seriously."

"In Europe, it's different – you eat soccer, you breathe soccer, you drink soccer. Everything is about soccer"

"If we knew that the goal lead (assassination of Colombian Escobar) against it, would rather have lost that game"

Thomas Helmer

"You have to stand up and be counted"

"I support the charity because it is up to people like me to take responsibility"

Tim Cahill

"Even as a really young kid, when it was a fairly unusual thing to be able to do. My family, being Samoan, loved rugby and because it is a fearless culture, I was encouraged simply to stick my head in anywhere, even when the boots were flying. People always talked about my lack of height, but I believe I showed them that how tall you are does not matter. It is the size of your heart that counts"

Tim Howard

"We're not bothered what anyone says. Put a ball out there, put 11 versus 11, and we want to win. It doesn't matter what the competition is"

"I knew he (Eddie Johnson) was nervous. I was nervous for him"

Titi Camara

"If it was a question of money, I could have stayed at Liverpool and picked it up. I need to play, and if I don't it is totally pointless"

"Every time I feel sorry for myself I just take a look at my standard of living and count my money. I'm playing football and I'm loaded"

Tomasz Radzinski

"I'd love to sign for Everton. They are offering me a wonderful four year deal, I could earn three times as much as I do know at Anderlecht. I know Everton are not a top club, they don't play in Europe"

"I won't have a lot of vacation time which is important for me with a new baby and all"

Tommy Docherty

"After the match an official asked for two players to take a dope test. I offered the ref"

"One of George Best's problems was he was a light sleeper. When it got light he went home and went to sleep"

"I've always said there's a place for the press but they haven't dug it yet"

Tommy Langley

"Fernando Torres is playing out of his face at the moment"

Tommy Smith

"Is that the German coach (Joachim Löw) or someone out of Depeche Mode"

Toni Polster

"Best regards to my father, my mother and especially, to my parents"

"Looking back, I think I must have done a lot of things right"

"There is a smear campaign against me with facts, which are not true"

Tony Adams

"Play for the name on the front of the shirt and they will remember the name on the back"

Tony Cascarino

"He's a good footballer, as in technical-wise"

Tony Cottee

"The thing about goalscorers is that they score goals"

Tony François

"Small details can make a big difference"

Tony Gale

"When you're there, it's one of those 'I was there' moments"

Tony Meola

"When I was ten years old I used to sit around and draw up designs for goalkeeper gloves and jerseys and now I am actually doing it. I couldn't be more excited"

Tony Pulis

"If we'd have scored, it would have been a different result"

Tranquillo Barnetta

"The Bundesliga is a different business"

"As a player, you always think that, you could help on the field more"

"It is pointless playing against the so-called small nations just to build up self-confidence"

Trevor Francis
"If that ball had dropped to a West Brom player, who'd put it in the net, that would have been the equaliser"

"The Scots have really got their hands cut out tonight"

Trevor Brooking

"It's end to end stuff, but from side to side"

"We don't get a second chance. We've already played them twice"

Trond Sollied

"I don't let my players do forest runs, because there are no trees on the pitch"

"Our goalscoring is like ketchup, you never now how much is going to come out of the bottle"

"If you buy with peanuts, you get monkeys, not football players"

"When the other team has the ball, we don't have the ball"

Ugo Ehiogu

"I´m as happy as I can be, but I´ve been happier"

Ulises de la Cruz

"Football has given me so much, has enabled me to do so much. So how can I help? That's what gives a meaning to my life"

Uwe Seeler

"I remember once asking Fritz Walter how mad you'd have to be to keep playing at 50, but seeing as I kept going until the age of 61 I'm sure you are getting an idea of how sane I am."

Vahid Halilhodžic

"It is better to win ten times 1-0 than to win once 10-0"

Vasilis Torosidis

"We hope to meet all our goals"

Vince Overson

"This club isn't a sleeping giant - it's more like a comatose dwarf"

Vicente Del Bosque

"We will send some signals to the country that we are going in the right direction. And if the success can be transferred into society, that would be marvellous"

Victor Dobrecovs

"Everything seen on the scoreboard. We're sitting at home"

Vincent Kompany

"I think a part of the reason why a lot of young kids fail is because they don't have the support from home that they need to"

"I've always kept myself occupied outside of football. That's my drive and that's what makes me better"

"History forgets when it repeats itself"

"You win the mental war when you have success"

Vinny Jones

"Winning doesn't really matter as long as you win"

Vittorio Pozzo

"How terrible it is when you lost, and how beautiful is football when you win"

"English players can be treated collectively. Italians have to be treated individually. They like to know that you're on their side"

Vladimir Beschastnykh

"Believe it or not, but sometimes lately I support the opposing team. I hope that after our next defeat they sack Benitez. But unfortunately it's not likely to happen as our club president likes him very much"

Vladimir Jugovic

"The problem with us foreigners is that we always learn to use the rude words first"

Vujadin Boškov

"Winning is better than a draw - and draw is better than losing"

"Football is unpredictable because all matches start zero to zero"

"Football is football"

Walter Casagrande

"I'm used to. Whenever the team goes bad, it's me who goes"

Walter Ayoví

"I still don´t know what my future holds"

Wayne Rooney

"Football is made up of all kinds of conflict"

"I lie in bed the night before the game and visualize myself scoring goals or doing well. You're trying to put yourself in that moment and trying to prepare yourself, to have a ´memory´ before the game"

"I am not the first player to have sworn on TV and I won't be the last"

Wesley Sneijder

"Leaving Madrid is not a defeat. They have treated me very bad"

Wilf McGuinness

"I like a drink as much as the next man - unless, of course, the man next to me happens to be George Best"

William Gallas

"It is cheating (WC 2006 Final), but they are Italians"

"Today our opponents tremble at the base when they see the formation of our team for the World Cup"

Willy Sagnol

"When I watch the English goals on television I sometimes feel that the strikers play in defence"

Wynton Rufer

"Even if it means parking the bus, fine. If we park the bus, get the strikers and wingers running their socks off, you can get a result"

Xavi Hernandes

"People who haven't played don't always realize how hard that is. Space, space, space. It's like being on the PlayStation. I think damn, the defender's here, play it there. I see the space and pass. That's what I do"

Xherdan Shaqiri

"I have proved that I am able to decide games. I had to earn respect"

"I am aware that I can never please everyone"

Yang Chen

"For a football player, nothing can match reaching the World Cup"

Yasser Al-Qahtani

"I have achieved many dreams and won many titles with the national team and it was an honour to wear the shirt"

Yasuhiko Okudera

And he (Otto Rehhagel) told me we'd be playing a zonaldefence. I'd never imagined I'd have to learn that"

Yassine Chikhaoui

"Health is the most important, everything else is coming after"

Yossi Benayoun

"We played like a bunch of drunks"

Young Chimodzi

"We took criticism as sportsmen"

Youssef Dahha

"For the goalkeepers, you need to be perserverant, courageous, driven and a hard worker. Always be ready to take challenges and show character"

Zdenek Zemen

"Referees don't make mistakes - Or at least they don't since I got fined for saying otherwise"

Zetti

"In sporting terms I was very good with my hands"

"It's not a job for just anyone. You stand there in goal, all alone, while players fire missiles at you"

"I also used to play outfield, but I was never picked there as I was hopeless!"

Zeze Moreira

"We did not come to Europe play the 'globetrotters'"

"Tele (Santana) revolutionized football"

Zico

"He (Romario) thinks he is the king of black coconut candy. What to expect from a guy who thinks he is a God?"

"My generation was not born to be world champion"

Zinedine Zidane

"I have won many awards and I am very happy about this, but I am not the best player in the world"

"I know what poverty is. I, too, lived in difficult places. And today I want to help. There are things in this world that are more important than football"

"You can't get bored of winning"

"Pressure is something that goes with football nowadays. You need to accept it, and everything that it involves - the good and the bad"

"They were very personal things that affected my mother and my sister . When you listen once, goes away. And so I did. But when he kept saying , twice, three times... The words struck me that there is more deep. First of all I am a man and would have rather been punched in the face"

"Life is full of regrets, but it doesn't pay to look back"

"Sometimes words are harder than blows"

Zizinho

"When mister Reader (referee) blew the final whistle, I looked to the side and I saw Obdulio (Varela) going crazy and start to doing cartwheels, I wanted to kick him"

Zlatan Ibrahimovic

"I don't need the Ballon d'Or to know I'm the best. It matters more to some players"

"What Carew (John) does with a football, I can do with an orange"

"First I went left, he (Stephane Henchoz) did too. Then I went right, and he did too. Then I went left again, and he went to buy a hot dog"

"One thing is for sure, a World Cup without me is nothing to watch"

"Gerrard has good skills, unlike normal English players"

"We were looking through his playlist in the dressing room – there was lots of Justin Bieber, Jonas Brothers and Selena Gomez. We were expecting some cool English rock bands and hip hop. It is nice to know that even David Beckham doesn't have good taste in everything"

"An injured Zlatan is a pretty serious thing for any team"

"Then Guardiola started his philosopher thing. I was barely listening. Why would I? It was advanced bullshit about blood, sweat and tears, that kind of stuff"

"I didn't injure you (Rafael Van der Vaart) on purpose, and you know that. If you accuse me again I'll break both your legs, and that time it will be on purpose"

"Now I'm here, I think the people in Paris will have something else to see besides the Mona Lisa"

"It's true that I don't know much about the players in Ligue 1 but for sure, they know who I am"

Zlatko Zahovic

"I can buy you (Srecko Katanec), I can buy your house, your family and I can buy that mountain we were running on in Slovenia during our preparations!"